www.wadsworth.com

www.wadsworth.com is the World Wide Web site for Thomson Wadsworth and is your direct source to dozens of online resources.

At *www.wadsworth.com* you can find out about supplements, demonstration software, and student resources. You can also send email to many of our authors and preview new publications and exciting new technologies.

www.wadsworth.com
Changing the way the world learns®

The Four Skills of Cultural Diversity Competence

A Process for Understanding and Practice

Third Edition

Mikel Hogan

California State University, Fullerton

THOMSON

BROOKS/COLE

Australia • Brazil • Canada • Mexico • Singapore • Spain • United Kingdom • United States

THOMSON

BROOKS/COLE

The Four Skills of Cultural Diversity Competence: A Process for Understanding and Practice, Third Edition

Mikel Hogan

Executive Editor: *Lisa Gebo*
Acquisitions Editor: *Marquita Flemming*
Assistant Editor: *Monica Arvin*
Editorial Assistant: *Samantha Shook*
Technology Project Manager: *Inna Fedoseyeva*
Marketing Manager: *Caroline Concilla*
Project Manager, Editorial Production: *Christy Krueger*
Creative Director: *Rob Hugel*
Art Director: *Vernon Boes*
Print Buyer: *Karen Hunt*

Permissions Editor: *Joohee Lee*
Production Service: *Rajendu Bhattacharya, Interactive Composition Corporation*
Copy Editor: *Melissa Messina*
Cover Designer: *Nina Lisowski*
Cover Image: *Pierre Tremblay / Masterfile*
Cover Printer: *Thomson West*
Compositor: *Interactive Composition Corporation*
Printer: *Thomson West*

Printed in the United States of America
1 2 3 4 5 6 7 10 09 08 07 06

For more information about our products, contact us at:
Thomson Learning Academic Resource Center
1-800-423-0563

For permission to use material from this text or product, submit a request online at http://www.thomsonrights.com.
Any additional questions about permissions can be submitted by email to
thomsonrights@thomson.com.

Thomson Higher Education
10 Davis Drive
Belmont, CA 94002-3098
USA

Library of Congress Control Number:
2005937464

ISBN 0-495-00779-X

To my children, grandchildren, and the children of the world

Contents

Chapter 3

Chapter 4

Chapter 5

Appendix

List of Tables, Figures, and Worksheets

Preface

The Four Skills of Cultural Diversity Competence introduces a process that opens the reader to growth in intercultural skills. It conducts the reader through an educational training program specifically designed to initiate and provide ongoing preparation for effective interaction with everyone in our rich cultural diversity. Growth in these skills equips individuals with the social and emotional grace they need to form the bonds of mutual trust and confidence that will bridge the differences that ordinarily divide people.

My life experience, growing up and living in Southern California, made it clear to me that intercultural skills grow only through information and practice. They seldom occur naturally in culturally diverse societies. I use some of my own childhood experiences to illustrate the theoretical premises of the educational and training process set forth in this book.

Although much of the United States can be described as culturally diverse, postwar Southern California is remarkable for the intensity and depth of its cultural diversity. It was in this rich multicultural setting during the 1950s and 1960s that the seeds of my awareness of the need for cultural understanding and skills were first sown.

Surprisingly, my learning began as a result of the absence of intercultural knowledge and skill rather than because of its practice. At that time, culturally diverse people, some of whom were minorities, lived in their own socially demarcated worlds, so intercultural communication was simply not happening. We did not enter into the process of shared information and effective interaction because we did not involve ourselves in intercultural relationships where intercultural communication could take place. To compound this situation further, we didn't even realize there was a problem. Woven into the very fabric of everyday life was the reality that black people lived in their part of the town,

Asian people in theirs, Latinos in theirs, and white Western Euro-American people in theirs. If anyone called attention to this state of affairs, our typical response would have been, "Where's the problem?" This is a classic example of cognitive blindness and its resultant denial.

The following story will help illustrate my point further. I grew up in a middle-class suburb, by and large Western European-American in its collective ethnicity. Within my community I regularly received quite contradictory cultural messages from my seemingly humanistic and liberal elders. For example, I heard such things as, "Don't worry about the clothes people wear or the color of their skin" and "all that matters is 'if you like them' as people." Yet when my brother and I suggested we bring home a black friend, we witnessed our parents recoiling in shock and fear. "We cannot bring Negroes here into our home, the neighbors won't like it; and we have to live in this neighborhood." I had thought that black/white racism stopped in the South and "fairness" reigned in the North. I was quite taken aback and confused at the mixed messages. It was not until later when I was in college that I reflected back on that incident and realized that racism and cultural intolerance began in my own home.

Sadly, such contradictions were the norm for me, and I saw this more clearly as the years passed. The words and behaviors I witnessed as a girl ranged from simple intolerance of difference to outright bigotry. My maternal Southern Baptist grandmother told me that "nigras" don't have souls, "so they can't go to heaven." There were the critical scowls and cutting disapproval of my Protestant grammar-school friends when confronted with my Irish Catholic practices. And then, in turn, those same friends would receive cruel grilling from my Irish Catholic paternal grandmother, when she was introduced to them and their names were anything but Irish: "Hmmm, my now, what's that name?" she would unashamedly ask them. "English? German? Why, there's no Irish in that name!" I remember the rude stares at the birthmark on my side whenever I wore a two-piece bathing suit to the beach and the startled responses and direct denials that even my name could generate. No one except my immediate family could believe that my name was really Mikel. "Why, that's a boy's name, after all," they'd say. Once my mother had to admonish the nuns at St. Anthony's when they insisted on calling me Michele.

My parents were, however naively, committed to education and cultural refinement, for themselves and their five children. When I was 13, they treated some of us to a fascinating and joy-filled six-week car tour of the length and breadth of Mexico. It was a fabulous trip, and one that I will never forget. But imagine my confusion after being exposed to the rich cultures of Mexico, to return to school only to hear the derisive comments about Mexicans—in a Catholic school with a substantial Latino population, no less. Later, I witnessed my family's grimaces and discomfort, and even denial, that my boyfriend (eventual husband) was Mexican American and the frequent discrimination we experienced in public when we went out as Mr. and Mrs. Garcia in the Los Angeles metropolitan area of the late 1960s.

When I was growing up, I was taught that regardless of race, color, ethnicity, creed, or other orientation, all that was really required for anyone to get on well in this land was hard work and an education, so for years I presumed a level playing field for all in the United States. Such notions of the existence of a great meritocracy formed the interpretive framework of my thinking, whatever the myriad contradictions I encountered in my daily life. And then there was Watts in 1965! The violence of this rebellion, for that is what it was, served to shatter any illusions I may have harbored about the myth of the great American meritocracy. No longer could I be told to "hush" or be put off with "well, that's different," because my experiences simply failed to match the myth.

By the late 1960s, in college, I found a fertile and tolerant ground to explore more freely the great puzzlement I felt about people and culture generally. Anthropology with its rich resource of cultural theories and concepts quite understandably captured and held my interest and won my devotion. The more I worked, the more I realized that this field offered the best approach for me to expand my understanding of culture and the human question. In college I became increasingly aware that throughout my life I had been marginalized, and it was through the use of the anthropological method of inquiry that I found a constructive way to explore that sense of marginality.

Anthropology as a discipline supplied the theoretical foundation for my work of exploration, but my investigation of diverse meanings and customs did not stop there. Beyond academic study and theory, my investigatory work took an active professional turn. Early on, my interests quite naturally led me into work with the Fair Housing Foundation of Long Beach. Later, I acted as program coordinator for Project Equity, a desegregation center located on the campus of Cal State University, Fullerton, that offered assistance to schools K–12. Through these affiliations I began working with the Coalition for Children, Adolescents, and Parents (CCAP) in the culturally diverse communities of Orange County. CCAP aimed to prevent teen pregnancy and other "at-risk" behaviors. Simultaneously, I founded the certificate program at Cal State University, Fullerton, entitled "Managing for Excellence with Culturally Diverse Employees and Customers" while continuing to teach university classes in anthropology and human services, always with an emphasis on race, ethnic, class, and gender relations.

Goal of This Book

It is in this developmental context that my own sense of cultural awareness and understanding took root and grew to include direct and specific problem solving in real communities as well as strategic planning in actual community development projects. These goals encompass something more than mere cultural awareness and understanding. My goals focus on cultural awareness and understanding that actually leads to the establishment of culturally effective techniques and processes that will routinely succeed in real communities. I have always aimed at cultural techniques and processes that succeed in real communities and that allow people to maintain pride in themselves, their cultures of origin, and any other groups or associations with which they regularly identify as they interact with others.

The specific techniques and processes I envision enable those who participate to appreciate another person's freedom to think and act differently. In other words, participants can agree to disagree. My techniques and processes enable participants to see that it is okay to differ, that difference is, in fact, something to be enjoyed. From difference itself, significant learning about oneself and one another eventually arises. These are the ground rules for productive interaction and exchange that effectively dissolve the sources of confusion, numbness, conflict, and festering animosity.

The Four Skills of Cultural Diversity Competence provides the reader with a step-by-step format for entering into and developing cultural competence. The process my book sets forth results from and draws strongly on my cultural diversity work over the past 25 years. It is based on a fundamental premise: Cultural competence is an ongoing and multilayered process that involves personal, interpersonal, and organizational levels—and is always in the moment.

Intended Audience

Because the book provides an adaptable four-skills approach to diversity competence development, it can be used by educators teaching in K–12 schools. Learning proactive ways of thinking about and communicating with diverse others is useful for preventing, defusing, and reducing conflicts at schools. Since there is a trend in colleges and universities to link academic education with job skills, this book is highly recommended to all courses in the social sciences and humanities. For example, the book can be used, as I use it, in human services and anthropology classes for promoting the integration of theory and practice into a needed and highly marketable job skill. In these classes I use the book as a supplement to the textbooks. See the sample syllabus in the Appendix.

Professional trainers and human resources personnel will also find the book useful in a range of work organizations: corporate training in business, nonprofit community agencies, government offices, schools, and medical facilities. The book serves as a stand-alone training workbook in these settings. The evaluations of my training workshops suggest reliability in the receptivity by workshop participants. For example, in one organization for which I have trained 1,564 people in 87 seminars, 90 percent of the participants rated the training "very good to excellent." I interpret these numerical indicators as suggesting reliability of the four-skills process. This is quite striking when one considers the rich cultural diversity of the training participants who write the evaluations. They are members of the many cultures that compose the Southern California community. People of every culture in the world live in Southern California. In fact, Los Angeles is called a "world city of cultures within cultures." And the four-skills training process is resonating well in this context.

How the Book Works: My Approach to the Subject

Being an anthropologist, I study human culture in its myriad forms: different ways of thinking and perceiving, different customs, and different communication systems and styles past, present, and everywhere in the world. Our communities are composed of people from diverse cultures who are thrust together in jobs, schools, and neighborhoods without effective ways of thinking or speaking across the diversity. To a great extent, people today are being placed into anthropological fieldwork situations without personal interest, training in cultural awareness, understanding, or communication skills.

I approach cultural diversity competence as multilevel. My approach encompasses cultural awareness, understanding, and skills at the personal, interpersonal, and organizational/institutional levels. The first two skills increase cultural awareness and understanding, and the third and fourth skills foster effective interpersonal skills, organization, and community change strategies. Each chapter combines both cognitive and experiential learning, and references for further exploration. Following adult learning principles, I assume cultural competence is acquired through a practice or dual exercise of action and reflection. With coaching, feedback, and self-reflection, in other words, one learns to be and to behave in a culturally competent manner.

Organization, Scope, and Content of the Third Edition

Every chapter has been updated with references, illustrations, and case examples derived from my university courses and training seminars in the occupational fields of education, social services, business, government offices, and medical facilities. Since I have been warned by many in the field that people do not "have time to read," I have tried to keep descriptions and explanations brief. To compensate for my brevity, however, I expanded the references for those interested in more topical information. In Chapter 1 I describe the context and need for cultural diversity competence as based in the very real change observed in our jobs and communities. In line with this context and need I then offer an overview of the four-skills development process. Chapter 2 introduces and demonstrates Skill One: Understanding Culture as Multilevel. Chapter 3 does the same with Skill Two: Understanding Common Barriers to Effective Relationships. Together, Skills One and Two form the "cultural-mindedness" that is the foundation for effective interactions, the subject of Chapter 4. In Chapter 4, Skill Three is introduced and demonstrated: Practicing Culturally Centered Communication Skills. We move on to Skill Four in Chapter 5: Designing Organizational Strategies and Action Plans, useful in organizations and in community outreach and change projects. Each chapter provides worksheets and discussion sheets designed to demonstrate the information presented on the four skills.

Learning Aids, Pedagogical Strategies, and Other Features

In each chapter, worksheets accompany presentation of each skill. The Instructor's Manual, available separately to instructors, includes brief pedagogical explanations, overhead transparencies, study and exam questions for each chapter, as well as assessment instruments. Since the first edition, the Internet has become an increasingly important means of communication. I have added suggestions for finding relevant websites in the References section featuring information on the field of cultural diversity competence. In addition, there is a book companion website that includes a glossary, chapter outlines, chapter summaries, key terms, websites, and chapter PowerPoint slides.

Acknowledgments

I thank my artist son, Michael J. Garcia, for transforming the four skills concepts into images, and I thank the many students and training participants for teaching me about the complexity of cultural diversity competence.

Chapter 1

Introduction

Cultural Diversity Competence: A Proactive Response to Change and Cultural Complexity

Current Context and Need for Cultural Diversity Competence

In recent years, the need for cultural diversity awareness and skill in the workplace and community has grown. Cultural awareness, coupled with the skills needed to interact successfully with people of diverse cultural backgrounds living and working in the same place, is called *diversity competence, cultural competence,* or *cultural diversity competence*. These terms imply the underlying qualities of awareness, understanding, and interpersonal skill (Arvizu, 2001; Bach, 1993; Barak, 2000; Chattopadhyay, 2003; Chung & Bemak, 2002; Coleman, 1990; Fontes, 2005; Foster et al., 1988; Hudson Institute, 1987; Kochan et al., 2003; Koppelman, 2005; Lamphere, 1992; Mackelprang & Salsgiver, 1999; Pederson, 1988; Tatum, 1997; Winkelman, 2005).

Often, the cultural awareness and skills that make people *diversity competent* are lacking today in a time when these qualities are most needed. Without cultural awareness and skills, operational gridlock can occur at great cost to the workplace and community. This situation has stimulated the concern of people engaged in business, education, health, and human services, and their concern has led to an increasing emphasis on the formal training of employees in cultural diversity competence in an effort to create culturally competent organizations. Culturally competent organizations have congruent structures, policies, programs, protocols, and processes that enable the entire system to work effectively with culturally diverse people (Carter, 2003; Coleman, 1990; Gardenschwartz & Rowe, 1998; Goldstein & Leopold, 1990; Hepburn, 2004; Kundu, 2003; Kurowski, 2002; Nash, 2001; Nelson, 1988; Richard et al., 2003; Susser, 2001; Thomas, 1996; Winkelman, 2005).

In the economic restructuring of the 1970s and 1980s, researchers Donald Schon (1987) and Ralph Killman (1987) explained that we as a nation no longer live in a "steady state" but in an "era of dynamic complexity." As a result, it has become a strategic imperative to adapt by instituting flexible and synergistic, that is, culturally competent—internally cooperative and fully inclusive—organizations and institutions in our whole sociocultural system. Killman states:

> Creating and then maintaining organizational success is a different kind of problem from that of only a few decades ago. The world has grown increasingly complex—resulting from the greater interdependence among world economies. At the same time the world has become increasingly dynamic—resulting from the information explosion and worldwide communications. This 'dynamic complexity' means that organizations cannot remain stable for very long. *Rather, constant change on the outside requires constant change on the inside.* Success is largely determined by how well the organization adjusts all its tangible and intangible properties to keep itself on track with its surroundings. (1987, pp. 2–3; *italics added*)

Adapting to ongoing economic and sociocultural changes means transforming our organizations and institutions into more flexible, collaborative systems that are "proactive," or anticipatory, cooperative, and timely rather than merely hierarchical and reactive. When our organizations and institutions become culturally competent in this way, they continually restructure themselves in response to unpredictable and constantly changing environments (Barak, 2000; Batteau, 2000; Carter, 2003; Hamada & Sibley, 1994; Jordan, 1994; Kanter, 1977, 1983, 1989; Killman, 1987; Kundu, 2003; Morgan & Ramirez, 1983; Richard et al., 2003; Schon, 1987; Schwartzman, 1993; Wright, 1994). Organizations and institutions cannot be culturally competent unless employees at every level develop cultural understanding and appropriate communication skills—*cultural competence*. This development allows for the emergence of collaborative, interdependent, or team relationships that in turn provide the foundation for synergistic, culturally competent organizations and institutions. These organizations are capable of producing strategies on an ongoing basis that proactively respond to diverse and changing economic, social, and political environmental conditions.

To ensure the development of culturally competent organizations, everyone involved must develop modes of interacting with one another that value diversity and anticipate change. These modes of interacting foster understanding among people, which is one of the basic dynamics in the development of teamwork. Teamwork, or synergy, is possible only if people treat one another with respect and communicate with one another in ways that form bonds of mutual

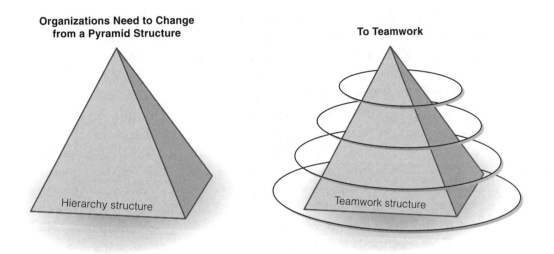

FIGURE 1.1 Organizations Need to Change to Teamwork Structure

trust. This is the challenge in the workplace, in communities—and for all of humankind: to design effective strategies to meet the reality of ever increasing cultural diversity in the midst of constant change (Arvizu, 2001; Barak, 2000; Eddy & Partridge, 1987; Kogod, 1994; Thomas, 1996; Winkelman, 2005; Wulff & Fiske, 1987). A visual representation of the traditional and teamwork organization is in Figure 1.1.

Cultural diversity itself is a challenge that has faced us since our nation's inception and continues to do so. Approached from a proactive stance, it provides a rich resource for fresh ideas and alternative ways of approaching people and offers significant points of contact with virtually all the nations of the world. This human resource provides us with the practical means for developing flexible and creative strategies for timely responses to environmental change as well. In this sense, cultural diversity becomes the foundation upon which we can rest our hopes for a successful future and for better success in managing our business affairs, educating our children, and surviving on this small planet. At this stage, business, education, and survival are vitally linked (Bodley, 2001; Koppelman, 2005; Winkelman, 2005).

To use the rich human resource of our cultural diversity, competence in this area becomes essential. This book defines **cultural diversity competence** as the ability to function with awareness, knowledge, and interpersonal skill when engaging people of different backgrounds, assumptions, beliefs, values, and behaviors. This text offers a practical hands-on process for developing four basic skills of cultural diversity competence relevant to personal, interpersonal, and organization-wide levels.

Developing the Four Skills of Cultural Diversity Competence: An Overview of the Training/Learning Process

Multilevel Challenges

The cultural challenges facing our society are multilevel: personal, interpersonal, organizational, and institutional. Therefore, the training model designed to address them must be multilevel as well. I refer to such a multilevel model as systemic and holistic because it addresses and encompasses the multilevel whole. That is, the systemic and holistic training model guides individuals in learning how to recognize and value diversity in themselves and in the people with whom they interact (micro level). As it fosters the growth of respect between individuals and expands the ability to communicate effectively within diverse work and community environments, the training process fosters change at the organization or meso level. As organizations become culturally competent through this process, change at the institutional or macro level is fostered (see Figure 1.2).

The broad objective of this training model is to work on a person-to-person basis to provide an interpersonal foundation for change while refashioning our hierarchical social structures into more collaborative, synergistic organizations. Such organizations base themselves on teamwork and have proven to be less wasteful of personnel than their hierarchically structured counterparts (Arvizu, 2001; Barak, 2000; Dodd & Taylor, 2005; Eisler, 2002; Fernandez, 1991; Hepburn, 2004; Jamieson & O'Mara, 1991; Kanter, 1977, 1983, 1989; Kogod, 1994; Loden, 1996; Loden & Rosner, 1991; Morgan & Ramirez, 1983; Morrison, 1992; Rosener, 1998; Schein, 1996; Thomas, 1996).

Table 1.1 presents the stages in a model of organization-wide cultural competence I used in 2002 after I had trained all employees of a social services organization in the four skills presented in this book. The stages listed provide a visual progression of "next steps" for organization-wide planning.

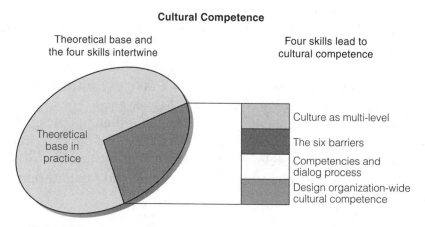

FIGURE 1.2 Overview of Cultural Competence Four Skills

Table 1.1 *Action Plan Process to Illustrate Holistic Model of Organization Change*

Action Plan Stages of Organization Change Process 2002

1st Stage: Identify the Organization's Needs
- The four-skills training guides the development of employee cultural awareness and capacity to engage in organization-wide cultural competence needs assessment.

2nd Stage: Increase Awareness, Understanding, and Skills of all Employees
- Training on four skills of cultural competence presents and demonstrates four measurable skills.
- Employee training on cultural competence provides information on obstacles to cultural competence identified by all employees and contributes to the needs assessment.
- The four-skills training of all employees provides the foundation for an organization-wide cultural competence implementation plan (action or strategic plan).

3rd Stage: Strategic Plan (Develop Strategies and Implementation Plan)
- Employees develop action plans useful in strategic planning for implementing a culturally competent organization. Strategies are contained in Chapter 5 of *The Four Skills of Cultural Diversity Competence.*

4th Stage: Monitor Progress on a Regular Basis with Measurable Objectives and Timelines
- Employee action plans contain measurable objectives and timetables useful for this stage.

Anthropological Fieldwork Principles Guide the Process

This training model derives from several dynamic anthropological principles of fieldwork, the goal of which is understanding human beliefs and behaviors past and present. It grounds itself in self-reflection and nonjudgment, emic contextualization and comparison, and the implementation of change through a holistic approach (Hogan-Garcia, 1991, 1995). Briefly stated, self-reflection and nonjudgment are active processes of understanding oneself and others over one's life span while suspending judgment. Anthropologists call this orientation *cultural relativism.*

Self-reflection and nonjudgment allow us to grow in our awareness and understanding of the ways our psychobiological capabilities of perception, memory, emotions, and symbolic processes interact with, and are influenced by, the sociocultural contexts of our daily lives over time. This orientation requires us to work constantly at understanding the ways in which our daily identity and sense of self are influenced by the sociocultural milieu in which we work and live.

Emic contextualization and comparison form the process of obtaining information on attitudes, value orientations, and social relations directly from the people involved in the situation at hand—from the insiders (called "emic" in anthropological fieldwork). This process requires continuous, mutually respectful contact with others in the work of participant observation and interviewing, in the gathering of life and family histories, for example. It is an attempt to enter the mental world of others, to experience the categories and logic by which others see the world, and to see the content and pattern of their daily existence. This approach relies on a human interactive mode that pays close attention to culture, comparisons, insider viewpoints, and accountability to the self and others.

A holistic or systems approach to cultural competence employs serious systemwide planning, implementation, and evaluation of organization policies and procedures in relation to organization goals—in this case, cultural diversity competence. The holistic approach also requires scrutiny of the organization from within the political and economic context of the wider sociocultural system of which the organization is a part (Hannerz, 1992, pp. 62–99; Haviland, 2005; Lavenda & Schultz, 2000, pp. 14–26).

These dynamic anthropological principles correspond to the personal, interpersonal, and organizational levels that typically encounter barriers blocking effective human relations and communication within hierarchically ordered organizations. The task is to gain understanding of human cultural diversity and to translate the cultural understanding into behaviors respectful of people, as well as to the organization policies that govern daily life.

The training model presented in Table 1.2 consists of three columns: the anthropological principles, cultural knowledge, and actions/skills. One's cultural knowledge, column 2, and one's actions/skills, column 3, which include verbal and nonverbal communication skills, are interdependent. These components are also multilevel in that they flow

Table 1.2 *Multilevel Training Model for Implementing Cultural Diversity Competence*

Apply Anthropological Principles ↔*	Obtain Cultural Knowledge ↔	Practice Actions/Skills ↔
1st Level:		
Personal Level of Change Process: Practice Self-Reflection and Nonjudgment	Personal Culture (Core Identity)	Practice 14 Personal Competencies (see Chapter 4)
2nd Level:		
Interpersonal Level of Change Process: Practice Emic Contextualization and Comparison	Specific Cultures: • U.S. National Culture • Subcultures • Organization Cultures	Obtain Accurate Cultural Information through Dialogue, Conflict Recovery, and Problem Solving (see Chapter 4)
3rd Level:		
Organization Level of Change Process: Holistic/Systemwide Approach	Organization Culture: • Policies • Programs • Procedures • Processes	Devise Action Plans and Organization-wide Strategies (see Chapter 5)

*The double arrows mean all three areas are interrelated and reinforce each other.

directly from the anthropological principles previously discussed and shown in column 1. Columns 2 and 3 can be viewed as an experiential application of the principles. Therefore, Table 1.2 schematically represents the organization's holistic systems approach to change. Namely, it encompasses each individual's work at self-reflection and nonjudgment as well as interpersonal emic contextualization and comparison for understanding, and it devises problem-solving or prevention strategies for organization-wide change.

The outcome of this complex and combined effort is:

1. cultural diversity competence at the individual level because obtaining cultural knowledge increases cultural awareness and understanding of self and others

2. effective relationships at the interpersonal level because participants practice interpersonal skills based on the expanded cultural understanding they have each achieved

3. culturally competent organizations at the systems level because organization-wide cultural competence can then be implemented through strategic action planning devised with the input of all employees

Change at the Individual Level: A Model

Change at the individual level is a process of self-reflection involving the actualization of the 14 competencies, or personal-level skills for change (Skill Three), a subject I address in Chapter 4. This involves a twofold dynamic of recognition and the subsequent modification of personal behavior. This change takes place within the mind and behaviors of the individual as the organization or community is in the process of change. I think of this self-reflective behavioral change process in terms of gradations in the intensity, duration, and frequency of the individual's recognitions and behavior modifications. Oftentimes, the process is one of taking two steps forward and one step back. Because cultural diversity competence is an interpersonal skill, acquiring it is a continuous process. The more we practice diversity competence skills, the sharper these skills become and the more spontaneously we behave in culturally competent ways.

Change at the Organizational Level: A Model

When working with evolving organizations, or organizations in the process of change, I find it helpful to envision the process taking place in four stages. Stage 1 is a stage of *relative equilibrium*. The organization functions in a relatively smooth manner until some factor, such as a marked increase in employee diversity, destabilizes its functionality. As the intensity of conflict increases, due to lack of understanding and mis-communication, the organization enters Stage 2, sometimes referred to as "the storming stage." Stage 2 is a critical stage. The organization can remain mired in pervasive conflict where *reaction,* as the interpersonal process employed, becomes the norm, resulting in a state of ongoing organizational dysfunction. However, if the organizational leadership demonstrates awareness and vision by implementing *proactive* processes in the form of diversity-competence training for employees, members of the organization can learn to work together successfully through any crisis. Stage 3 is the ability to work through problems proactively. It is called the *proactive problem-solving stage.* And Stage 4 is the attainment of a new relative equilibrium (Rosen, 1991; Smith, 1993).

Interactive Learning Mode

The interactive learning mode of my four-skills approach combines both cognitive and experiential learning. Following adult learning principles, cultural competence is acquired through the practice of action and reflection. Put simply, with coaching, feedback, and self-reflection, the individual learns to behave in a diversity-competent manner by carrying out diversity-competent actions (Brookfield, 1990; Hogan-Garcia, 1991; Kohls, 1984; Mehr, 1992; Paige, 1993; Sikkema & Niyekawa, 1987; Winkelman, 2005). Toward this end, my formula is:

PRESENTATION + DEMONSTRATION + PRACTICE + DEBRIEFING (PDPD) = TRAINING

Presentation usually entails the use of visuals such as PowerPoint and allows ample time for questions that may follow. **Demonstration** can consist of films and case analysis. **Practice** can involve any of various exercises, role-playing and cultural simulations being notable examples. Structured **debriefing** allows participants to discuss their experience of the foregoing components in three ways:

- in terms of what they learned about themselves personally
- in terms of what they learned about others
- in terms of learning how they can apply their knowledge in practical life experiences

Structured debriefs are included at the end of each learning activity in the chapters that follow because it is an important aspect of the learning process (Cryer, 1987; Johnson, 1992; Thatcher, 1990; Van Ments, 1992).

Table 1.3 represents the stages individuals and organizations attain as they become culturally competent individuals and organizations. The actual process is an organic one in which the stages interrelate dynamically in a forward-and-back, overlapping manner. Individuals growing culturally competent provide the human infrastructure for developing culturally competent organizations because the norms,

Table 1.3 *Cultural Diversity Competence Change Process*

Stages	Levels
1st	Self-Reflection (personal awareness and understanding)
2nd	Personal Competencies (14 personal behavioral skills)
3rd	Diversity-Competent Individuals (interpersonal level)
4th	Effective Teamwork (interpersonal and group level)
5th	Culturally Competent Organizations (respect and proactively use cultural diversity)

policies, procedures, programs, and processes of such organizations reflect to what levels they value and use cultural diversity.

Chapter Summary

In this chapter, I have described what cultural diversity competence is and why it is essential. My conclusions are based on the increasing, observable changes in organizations and institutions in this country and in the world. I then offer an overview of my training process to implement proactive, holistic programs to respond to these circumstances of culture change. The model is holistic because it is multilevel: personal, interpersonal, systemwide. The model, furthermore, is based on anthropological field methods honed by living side by side and participating with the people of the world for extended periods in an effort to understand their beliefs and behaviors (culture) from their perspective. Moreover, I describe preliminary models for change, not only on the individual level but on the organizational level as well. I conclude with a discussion of the practical, interactive nature of the training process presented in this book.

In Chapter 2, I introduce and demonstrate Skill One, understanding culture as multilevel.

Worksheet 1

Context and Need: Identifying Change and Diversity (approx. 20 minutes)

Worksheet 1 will help you experience, in a direct fashion, your own personal observations regarding change in cultural diversity.

Purpose: To demonstrate current context of population diversity and the fast pace of change and to promote a recognition of the need for cultural competence.

Instructions: Form groups of two to four persons. Discuss question 1, and list pertinent examples for the item. If you are in a web-based online course, reflect on the answer to the question and list your examples.

1. Have you witnessed any examples of change related to cultural diversity in the last two years? Please list. (approx. 10 minutes)

Examples: Computer systems regularly updated and changed by the university throughout the campus because of continuing developments in computer hardware and software. Or, with respect to cultural diversity, the continuing increase of students in my classes from Russia, Romania, Bosnia, Croatia, Ethiopia, and Afghanistan.

Your Example:

_____

_____

_____

_____

Debriefing Questions

Write your answers to the debriefing questions individually in the spaces that follow. Discuss as a group as time and circumstance allows. (approx. 15 minutes)

Example:

1. Describe your personal reactions to doing this activity.

I realize I need to practice patience in relation to software and other technical changes.

2. What did you learn about yourself from this activity?

The use of computers is now an integral part of teaching and I need to stop grumbling about the need to routinely upgrade my computer skills.

3. What did you learn about others?

I observe a variety of faculty responses to the routine changes ("upgrades") in computer software. Some faculty resist using their computer altogether for e-mail and for instructional purposes. Other faculty upgrade their skills when they can (they muddle through), and others anticipate and embrace technical changes with gusto and a light heart.

4. Name two ways you can use this learning in daily life activities.

- I could regularly upgrade my computer skills by taking classes in the university's Faculty Development Center.

- I could enrich my classes and my technological skill by requiring students to participate in the online Discussion Forum on the course website.

Your Debriefing Questions

1. Describe your personal reactions to doing this activity.

2. What did you learn about yourself from this activity?

3. What did you learn about others?

4. Name two ways you can use this learning in daily life activities.

Worksheet 2

Teamwork Experience

Worksheet 2 will help you experience, in a direct fashion, your own personal observations regarding the dynamic aspects of teamwork.

Purpose: To reflect on and to recognize the process of teamwork.

Instructions: Briefly describe in the space below an example in which you worked as a member of a team or saw others work as a team. (approx. 10 minutes)

> **Example:** I serve as a member of the Steering Committee of California's Mental Health Services Act for the local county. Our task is to restructure the county's mental health services according to such principles as client centered, family focused, culturally competent, outcome driven, strengths based, comprehensive and integrated, individualized to client, coordinated care, least restrictive and most appropriate care, and programs and services that are evidence-based best practices (Mental Health Services Act, 2005). Because the committee members come from different academic disciplines and professions, which in itself creates a dynamic mix of different "professional cultures," the completion of our task requires we work cohesively across our differences.
>
> **Your Example:**
>
> _____
>
> _____
>
> _____
>
> _____

Debriefing Question

Write your answers to the debriefing questions individually in the spaces that follow. Discuss as a group as time and circumstance allow. (approx. 15 minutes)

1. Describe your personal reactions to doing this activity.

2. What did you learn about yourself from this activity?

3. What did you learn about others?

4. Name two ways you can use this learning in daily life activities.

Chapter 2
Skill One

Understanding Culture as Multilevel

The Concept of Culture

People usually apply a traditional definition to the concept of culture, one that assumes a stability, coherence, and homogeneity in the patterns of social groups and their behaviors. This kind of traditional definition, called *essentialism,* needs to be avoided because it can result in stereotyping and discrimination (Bashkow, 2004; Foley & Moss, 2001; Goode, 2001; Hill-Burnett, 1987; Orta, 2004; Rosenblatt, 2004). Leininger (1988) offers a more useful definition. She provides a dynamic multilevel definition of culture relevant to both group and individual levels. Her concept of culture is "learned, shared, and transmitted values, beliefs, norms, and lifeways of a group which are generally transmitted intergenerationally and influence one's thinking and action modes" (p. 9).

Thinking of culture in relation to two broad components helps us recognize it has both invisible and visible dimensions and it is vibrant and layered:

1. Culture is both subjective and objective.
2. Culture is multilevel and dynamic.

Culture as Subjective and Objective

Culture is both subjective and objective. Subjectively, culture is composed of a meaning system. Objectively, culture dictates how and why we behave in certain ways. The subjective aspect, beliefs, values, and explanatory cognitive frameworks that are communicated both verbally and nonverbally are learned through social interactions in the family and in the general social milieu and have a pervasive impact on everything we see and do. And, more important, the subjective aspects of culture remain largely invisible, unremarked, and unrecognized by the majority of human beings, similar to a fish being unaware of the water in which it lives. A metaphor by Geert Hofstede (1997) refers to this component of culture metaphorically as the "software of the mind." He draws on society's computer experience to convey, in a concrete and palpable way, the pervasive yet invisible influence of subjective culture on our thoughts and behaviors. Likewise, Edward and Mildred Hall (1987) use a computer simile to describe culture: "Culture can be likened to an enormous, subtle, extraordinarily complex computer. It programs the actions and responses of every person, and these responses must be mastered by anyone wishing to make the system work" (pp. 3–4).

Culture acts objectively as well. Its objective component is patterned behavior, transforming the word *culture* from noun to verb. For example, Bordieu describes the concept of "habitus," or the implicit patterns of subjective experience where the intersection of objective and subjective becomes apparent. He states, "The habits of practical mastery [habitus] . . . are not perceived by actors as arbitrary or the product of successive habituating experiences but as natural and self-evident . . . subjective experience is a pattern of organization . . . it is habituation to an unspoken rationale, inarticulate yet compelling because it is embodied in social interaction" (Partridge, 1987, p. 222). In this sense, culture then is a metatheory for explaining human behavior, particularly as it varies across groups (Bashkow, 2004).

Culture as Multilevel and Dynamic

In addition, culture operates on several levels simultaneously. Therefore, people need to think of it in these terms. Culture exists at the **micro level** of the individual—that is, in a person's assumptions, values, beliefs, explanatory systems, and behaviors, which are learned and shaped by the power relations in the family and other basic social groups. At the same time, culture exists at the **meso level** in the groups with which we identify and within which we interact. Each individual belongs to many groups based on ethnicity, gender, age, class, race, religion, sexual orientation, ableness, occupation, and region of the country. **Macro-level culture** refers to the structure and processes of organizations and societal institutions, most of which are stratified hierarchies. Culture, thus, encompasses our schools, workplaces, the media, our government, and the criminal justice system. The norms, programs, policies, and procedures of organizations and institutions reflect the culture in which and through which we live. This book's focus is four levels of culture: the personal level, ethnic or culture group level, mainstream national cultural level, and organizational/institutional culture level. Offering specific examples, each level becomes more familiar as we proceed.

Organizations and their cultures frame our daily lives. Our decisions and behaviors become the generative source of culture in the ways that norms are implemented and changed and in the ways that programs, policies, and procedures are interpreted and enacted by individuals. Organizations and their cultures thus provide our *generative matrix*. Anthropologist William Partridge states:

> In this view, culture is not a driving determinative force as much as it is a product of ongoing social interaction. It is only one resource, upon which actors draw in an ever-present process of recasting, reinterpreting, reinventing and revising culture so that it conforms to the needs of social practice then emerging. The result of this ever-present process of revision is the objective element of practice, and it exists as the product of prior social actions. Practical activity, then, is the generative act of cultural construction. (1987, p. 220)

Discussing the multilevel and dynamic properties of culture helps us recognize that culture exists both inside and outside us all. We understand that culture, although we have internalized it in the context of our social environment, is continuously shaped and perpetuated through our individual behaviors and choices (Handwerker, 2001; Haviland, 2005; Levinson, Foley, & Holland, 1996; Winkelman, 2001, 2005). In 1993, for example, the National Endowment for Humanities (NEH) initiated a program entitled "A National Conversation on American Pluralism and Identity." The intention of the NEH was to articulate perspectives on what it means to be an American. One of the outcomes of this program was the funding of a series of panel conversations at the Field Museum in Chicago. In seeking to translate an effective approach to culture and diversity to the public, the forum focused on "how values arise, shape our actions and are continually re-shaped by our social interactions" (Wali & Kahn, 1997). Clearly, therefore, through reflection and understanding, through our daily choices and the way we interact with others, we all possess the power to change our culture, at least at the personal level (DeWalt & DeWalt, 2002, pp. 6–15, 30–33; Hannerz, 1992).

Aspects of Culture

The following list of the aspects of culture is designed to work as a tool for observing and comparing culture in general, the learned and shared way of life all humans possess, with the specific cultures we encounter at work and elsewhere. The list provides a vocabulary for perceiving, recognizing, and discussing cultural differences and for obtaining the relevant information one needs to identify and solve problems through comparisons. Because cultural dynamics are often unrecognized and "invisible," a supple vocabulary is needed to bring culture into our awareness (Hogan-Garcia & Wright, 1989).

Culture in general or cultural universals refer to the customary ways by which humans live, since culture is at the core of human existence. The following aspects describe human culture broadly and, therefore, become holistic in terms of their inclusiveness facilitating the recognition of the equal humanity of all groups (Lavenda & Schultz, 2000, pp. 14–20).

In addition, the listing provides the basis for discussing the beliefs and customs of specific cultures, such as Mexican or Vietnamese cultures. The term *ethnic group* or *subculture* refers to the cultural heritage, or aspects of culture, that a group shares and attempts to hand down from one generation to the next through learning. The term *ethnic group* or *subculture* is one of many categories used in complex stratified societies such as the United States to distinguish social groups (other categories include age, class, race, gender, sexual orientation, disability). Ethnic groups maintain their cultural differences by means of isolating mechanisms such as geographic, social, political, and economic barriers. In other words, the aspects of the group's cultural beliefs, identities, practices, and boundaries are established by the members and by pressures from outsiders (Bashkow, 2004; Barth, 1968, 1998; Goode, 2001; Lavenda & Schultz, 2000, pp. 20–26, 88–89; Montagu, 1974).

The following list can be used to clarify culture at the four levels previously mentioned, the personal, ethnic or culture group, mainstream national, and organizational levels, as the worksheets at the end of the chapter demonstrate.

Twelve Aspects of Culture or Ethnicity

1. History
2. Social Status Factors
3. Social Group Interaction Patterns: Intragroup (within-group relations) and Intergroup (between-group relations)
4. Value Orientations
5. Language and Communication: Verbal and Nonverbal
6. Family Life Processes
7. Healing Beliefs and Practices
8. Religion
9. Art and Expressive Forms
10. Diet/Foods
11. Recreation
12. Clothing

History   A written or oral history that refers to the account of a particular group's collective experience in geographic place and time. The time period and conditions under which groups immigrated or migrated is significant when we consider that these factors influence their subsequent opportunities. The Irish in the 19th century, for example, entered North America when low-wage jobs were plentiful on farms and in cities. The Puerto Ricans, in the 20th century, came when the economy was contracting and fewer overall jobs were available. Moreover, having political/economic power influences whose history is written. Many people in the United States have never heard of the Luiseno Indians of Southern California because this culture is never written into the history books. In the case of the Luiseno, those who are aware of them may inaccurately assume they were all killed during the American Indian genocide that took place in the 19th century in Southern California (Carrico, 1987; Caughey, 1995; Heizer, 1974; Hurtado, 1988; Starr & Orsi, 2000).

Social Status   refers to one's social position, or "class," in society's hierarchy based on education, occupation, and income. This aspect of culture hinges on the nature of economic, political, and education institutions of the society. In the United States it is uncommon for many people to consciously recognize social class because of the pervasive belief in meritocracy, the conviction that the United States is a fair, color- and gender-blind society. The ideology of meritocracy serves to mask recognition of institutionalized inequalities.

Social Group Interaction Patterns   are the **social** relations within and between groups, although group boundaries are in reality fuzzy and changing as a result of political-economic factors.

   Intragroup relations are among members within the same group. These relations are influenced by age, gender, color, religion, education, socioeconomic background, sexual orientation, language or dialect spoken, and culture change (acculturation) processes, which can include culture shock and intergenerational conflict.

   Intergroup relations are between members of different groups. Social status and political-economic power is relevant here. Are relations cooperative and friendly or conflict ridden? Is there economic and political exploitation with widespread stereotyping and institutional discrimination? We explore six barriers to effective relations, within and between groups, in Skill Two in Chapter 3: verbal communication (language), nonverbal communication, preconceptions/stereotypes/discrimination, judgment, stress, and organization-wide barriers, based on internal organization norms.

Value Orientations   are the deep subjective ideals and standards by which members of a culture judge their personal actions and those of others. Individualism, competition, and consumerism are three values common to U.S. mainstream national culture.

Language and Communication   are composed of two components. **Verbal communication,** or language, includes the verbal categories and language structure (grammar and syntax) for the perception of reality and for communication among humans. **Nonverbal communication** refers to everything else that conveys meaning but primarily remains unconscious. Tone of voice, gestures, facial expression, touching, body smell, and time orientation are aspects of communication that convey meaning directly without the use of words. The experience of time is elusive and depends on the culture's time orientation of which we are a member. For example, tribal societies live in "eco-time," which is experienced as human centered: one's activities flow from one's personal pace and comfort level. Highly structured societies such as the Maya of Yucatan, Inca of Peru, Aztecs of Mexico, and the Chinese experienced time as "participatory cosmologies." Time in these cultures was experienced as controllable and its careful control through ritual was vital to the affairs of the state. Time in these cultures stands in stark contrast to the time orientation of the United States' national culture, in which we feel like "helpless bystanders" (Aveni, 2002; Gell, 1992). Worksheet 7 provides an activity relative to the time orientation of the United States' national culture.

However subtle, nonverbal communication is a potent factor in culturally and socially diverse settings and gives rise to much misunderstanding.

Family Life Processes   encompass gender, family, and occupational roles. Gender roles become an essential part of this aspect of culture in considering the spoken and unspoken rules for male and female behavior that vary greatly among the different cultures of the world. Also, occupation, education, marriage customs, divorce, and parenting beliefs and practices are included here. Family structure is relevant as well. *Nuclear family* is the term for father, mother, and children living in the same household. *Extended family* refers to a mix of relatives under the same roof. *Augmented family* and *recombined families* are terms to describe households in which one or both parents were previously divorced or widowed (Parkin & Stone, 2004; Stone, 2001).

Healing Beliefs and Practices   refer to the assumptions, attitudes, beliefs, and practices people possess regarding health, their bodies, determinants of disease, pain, death, and health practices and practitioners (Anderson, 1996; Culhane-Pera et al., 2003; Kleinman, 1988; Nebelkopf & Phillips, 2004; Spector, 2000).

Religion   corresponds to the myriad spiritual beliefs and practices of human cultures (Bowie, 2000; Lessa & Vogt, 2000; Pandian, 2002).

Art and Expressive Forms   involves the creative use of imagination in interpreting, understanding, and enjoying life. These forms include visual art, myth, ritual, stories, proverbs, poetry, ballads, legends, music, and performance art.

Diet/Foods are the preferred foods eaten by groups and their members. To many people, this aspect of culture is a quality-of-life issue.

Recreation refers to pastimes, activities, and sports for leisure and enjoyment.

Clothing are the types, styles, and extent of body coverings.

Personal Culture

Personal culture, often referred to as *core identity*, is a dynamic entirety that underlies one's individual behavior and includes everything an individual finds meaningful, beliefs, values, perceptions, assumptions, and explanatory frameworks about reality itself. Each individual possesses a complex identity. It is learned and is shaped by the power relations within the social interactions of family and others who live in our sociocultural milieu. As a person's sociocultural milieu typically changes over the course of a lifetime, likewise does one's personal identity. A good example comes to mind in my own personal culture. I grew up in suburban Southern California in a middle-class, Irish-Catholic family, the second of five children born in rather quick succession. Each of my siblings and myself demonstrate our own unique version of this upbringing. No two of us are identical and the interplay of our similarities, differences, and memories continues to evoke amazement.

Ethnicity influences personal identity as it intersects with other influences, including age, race, gender, ableness, religion, physical appearance, sexual orientation, and social economic position (Merry, 2001).

Personal Culture Change and the Stages of Sociocultural Awareness

The depth of the population's awareness of social stratification and of the assumptions that mainstream culture places on daily life stands out as a significant issue in the development of cultural diversity competence. Mainstream culture—that is, the national culture of the United States—by its monocultural assumptions and policies as implemented in schools, the media, and other institutions and organizations heavily influences the way we develop a sense of self. Moreover, our sense of self is overtly influenced by mainstream culture's mechanisms of stratification regarding age, race, ethnicity, gender, language, religion, sexual orientation, physical appearance, and degree of ableness. Embedded within the mechanisms of stratification, described more fully in Chapter 3, are five assumptions:

1. The United States is a meritocracy of equal individuals.
2. Americans don't have a culture.
3. If it is different, it is wrong or deficient.

4. One should never talk about cultural diversity.

5. One should never admit to being prejudiced (Tatum, 1993).

These mechanisms are ideological and institutionalized for the purpose of keeping people fixed on certain, oftentimes lower, rungs of the societal ladder. These rungs determine their access to resources and, therefore, the quality of life they enjoy. Furthermore, these stratifying mechanisms are activated and brought into play by many things outside one's control: ethnicity, race, age, gender, socioeconomic status, sexual orientation, and ableness (Baker, 2004; Essed, 1991; Ewen, 1998; Fine et al., 1997; Jones, 1992; Mackelprang & Salsgiver, 1999; Merry, 2001; Phinney & Rotherman, 1987; Tatum, 1993, 1997).

Even though people may not be conscious of them, mainstream culture's monocultural assumptions and stratification mechanisms profoundly affect the personality development of *everyone* living in this society. This means that we have all been schooled by mainstream U.S. culture to think about diversity in a certain way. As a result, most of us struggle at Stage 1 or 2 in the identity-change process, a subject I will now address.

It is not the purpose of this book to attempt a lengthy explanation of the identity-change process, a complex sociocultural and psychological phenomenon (Helms, 1989; Phinney & Rotherman, 1987; Phinney, 1989, 1990; Root, 1985, 1992; Winkelman, 2005). Nevertheless, it is important to mention the different stages of sociocultural awareness that occur in the identity-change process, because they manifest themselves in the interpersonal behaviors that arise in families, work domains, community, and other settings. The dynamics of the different stages profoundly affect interpersonal relations because they form barriers, such as stereotyping and negative judgment, to effective communication and relationships in culturally diverse settings. Therefore, the topic of personal identity in regard to the personal awareness of mainstream cultural assumptions and social stratification becomes central to the development of cultural competence. It directly relates to the personal and interpersonal barriers we establish in our workplaces and communities that give rise to the conflicts we experience daily, and, in this, the topic of personal identity is what makes this training program essential.

The stages of the identity-change process are integral to learning cultural diversity competence. An identity change implies a change in one's personal paradigm. Consequently, when individuals engage in a training process designed to sensitize them to such barriers as stereotyping and negative judgment, they emphatically begin addressing their personal paradigm: their meanings, beliefs, and deep assumptions about reality (Gochenour, 1993; Green, 1999; Paige, 1993; Winkelman, 2005). Furthermore, identity awareness and change, like all organic changes, do not take place in a neat sequential order, typical of the printed page or a visual aid. As an organic developmental process, identity changes that enhance cultural diversity competence are largely nonsequential and nonlinear. Although described as "stages," mainly for the purposes of presentation, participants can expect to find themselves taking two steps forward only to take one step back in the actual work. Finally, learning diversity competence requires new cultural information so that we can begin to perceive and think about cultural diversity in fresh and positive ways. New cultural information allows for the neutralization of negative emotional reactions that often attend identity change and the experience of cultural change and diversity in general. The aspects of culture presented earlier in this chapter are a tool for understanding culture, beginning with our own.

Let us then briefly review the identity-change stages as they relate to sociocultural awareness.

Identity-Change Stages

Stage 1: Conformity

Individuals at the stage of conformity do not recognize the impact that the meritocracy assumption or the denial of social stratification has on their lives. Preconceptions, stereotypes, confusion, stress, denial, or nonrecognition of sensitive issues related to diversity are the common characteristics of this stage (Loden & Rosener, 1991; Morrison, 1992; Winkelman, 2005).

Organizational norms, policies, procedures, and programs support and perpetuate the conformity stage in individuals. School curriculums and programs that lack components about cultural diversity also perpetuate the stage of conformity. They foster a monocultural perception and induce a kind of blindness to the current and historical reality of stratification and cultural diversity (Delgado & Stefancic, 1997; Koppelman, 2005; Sleeter & McLaren, 1995).

The remarks of Chris, a Euro-American man, when he viewed the first episode of the documentary *Eyes on the Prize*, nicely illustrates Stage 1:

> I never knew it [racism] was really that bad just 35 years ago. Why didn't I learn this in elementary or high school? Could it be that White people want to forget this injustice? . . . I will never forget that movie for as long as I live. It was like a big slap in the face. (Tatum, 1993, p. 7)

Stage 2: Resistance

At the stage of resistance, individuals question and resist anything that seems to contradict mainstream culture's assumptions and beliefs about diversity. Again, Beverly Tatum clearly illustrates the dynamics of this stage in the case of a Euro-American woman who, when exposed to information about racist policy during World War II, "felt anger and embarrassment in response to her previous lack of information about the internment of the Japanese Americans" (Tatum, 1993, p. 7).

Stage 3: Redefinition

Individuals at the stage of redefinition characteristically begin to redefine their identity in terms of the growing awareness and sensitivity they are discovering in themselves and the impact they see it having on their lives and the lives of others. At the end of one course on race, ethnic, and gender relations in America, students were asked to write about the personal effects of their coursework. The following selection of responses illustrates the stage of redefinition.

> I never realized how much "our" history books left out as to our involvement in the colonizing of other cultures.
>
> My view that women had progressed greatly in the workplace in terms of discrimination and sexual harassment was changed.
>
> I was unaware, until this semester, that the land and possessions of Japanese forced into concentration camps was not returned. It helped me understand why monetary compensation received by the Japanese several years ago was so important.
>
> The first racial paradigm of mine that was challenged was the continued harassment of Afro-Americans. I could not believe that this ethnic group still faces many obstacles in their path toward moving up in society. Another viewpoint of mine that was changed was the amount of sexual harassment in jobs and education. (Hogan-Garcia et al., 1991, pp. 88–89)

Stage 4: New Identity

Individuals at Stage 4 have begun to feel comfortable with the new identity they have achieved, based on the awareness and understanding of cultural and social diversity issues in the United States.

Stage 5: Diversity Competence

At Stage 5 individuals have achieved considerable growth in diversity competence and find themselves regularly able to develop effective relationships with people described as culturally and socially diverse (Foster et al., 1988; Helms, 1989; Sue, 1981; Tatum, 1993; Winkelman, 2005).

Subculture or Ethnic Groups and Race

A subculture or ethnic group is a group in which the members generally share a complex and dynamic common cultural heritage made up of the assumptions, values, beliefs, attitudes, and customs that relate to the aspects of culture we have been examining—that is, language, religion, family life processes, and so on. Each aspect involves and functions through associated values, beliefs, assumptions, and customary behaviors. In this way, culture or ethnic groups represent associated belief and behavior systems that are passed down from one generation to the next through learning. The beliefs and identities of members of ethnic groups are generated by its members and by pressures from outsiders, a process of survival for the culture. Ethnic or subculture groups exist within larger cultural systems. The United States, for example, has most cultures of the world living within its boundaries and each could be called an ethnic or subculture group.

With the exception of American Indians, who already lived for centuries in the Americas, and African Americans, who were brought against their will to the Americas, the United States is a nation of immigrants. This means that each of us is, to some extent, a member of a subculture or ethnic group. This is so even if we do not personally identify with that membership. The extent to which we identify with membership in an ethnic group varies according to a variety of circumstances, such as how we are treated, how many generations a family has been in the United States, whether one lives in an ethnic community, and how frequently we interact with members of our own ethnic community (Spector, 1996, pp. 1–75; Spector, 2000; Meador, 2005).

Again, my personal experience growing up in California as a child of fourth-generation Irish descent readily provides a convenient example of culture in the customs, beliefs, and common stories (all aspects of culture) I share with the individuals in my family group of origin. A second example comes from my personal experience of the Mexican heritage that I encountered in my marriage to a second-generation Mexican American from East Los Angeles, whose parents came from El Paso, Texas, and Chihuahua, Mexico. Common in Southern California, this kind of intermarriage introduces yet another layer of cultural complexity in the multicultural identities of our children, which aggravates the intersection of commonplace issues such as class differences among family members, color, age, degree of ableness, sexual orientation, and gender identity (Alba, 1990; Bashkow, 2004; Cyrus, 1998; Delgado & Stefancic, 1997; Lamphere, 1992; Ore, 2000; Phinney & Rotherman, 1987; Portes, 1996; Root, 1992; Winkelman, 1999, pp. 123–129; Winkelman, 2005; Zack, 1995).

The term *racial group* is also relevant because of the popular assumption and belief in separate races of humankind. As a result of historical social developments among groups in the United States, "race" is a sociocultural belief that ascribes differential status to groups of people within society based on physical differences, such as skin color and eye shape. Although race is commonly believed to be a biological classification of human groups, based on heredity and genetic differences, it has no scientific foundation. There is only one race of humans, and that is the human race (Cohen, 1998; Kottack & Kozaitis, 2003, pp. 84–120; Marks, 2005, pp. 1–7). I revisit this topic in Chapter 3.

U.S. Mainstream/National Culture and Hegemony

As a society, the United States is composed of a mainstream or national culture and numerous subcultures or ethnic groups. We name subcultures, for example, Mexican American, Irish American, African American, or Jewish American. National or mainstream culture has at its foundation a core culture that is English in origins and development (Fischer, 1989). Nevertheless, it has developed its own distinctive and unique expressions of the 12 general aspects of culture that I have been analyzing. (See "Aspects of Mainstream U.S. Culture" in the Appendix for this list.)

Mainstream or national culture is often referred to as the "dominant" culture. It is incorporated into, dominates, and informs all the major organizations and institutions of the United States. As a result, it is institutionalized in our societal structures. It is *hegemonic,* or in control in that it presides over all the various subcultures (Nader, 1994, 1996). Everyone needs to know how to recognize and be able to "dialogue" with the dominant culture in order to live and work comfortably and effectively within it, regardless of the subculture or ethnic group to which one may belong (Baker, 2004; Fine et al., 1997; Levinson et al., 1996; Sleeter & McLaren, 1995). I discuss mainstream culture's assumptions and beliefs concerning cultural diversity and race in Chapter 3 as well. For a pertinent example of an aspect of mainstream culture, please see the discussion of M-time in Worksheet 7. In addition, the Appendix contains a sketch of the "Aspects of United States Mainstream/National Culture."

Organization/Institutional Culture

Organization/institutional culture refers to the norms, policies, procedures, programs, and processes that organizations or institutions employ. Within each of these areas of organizational culture we find deeply embedded values, beliefs, assumptions, and customary ways of behaving, and inevitable contradictions (Eisler, 2002; Hamada & Sibley, 1994; Heyman, 2004, pp. 487–500; Jordan, 1994, 2003; Wright, 1994; Batteau, 2000). Using the list of the 12 aspects of culture as a guide, we can isolate and examine the various areas in organizational culture.

It is important and useful to be aware that organizational culture in the United States is highly congruent with mainstream or national culture, that organizational culture reflects and echoes mainstream culture in virtually every respect. A good example of this congruence lies within the phenomenon of the institutionalization of monochronic time orientation, perception, and the uses of time itself (see Worksheet 7). Consider another example: A "demanding" female supervisor of a human service agency demonstrates her unwarranted gender assumptions by regularly insisting that only men move and rearrange the office furniture and serve as bodyguards when the agency must deal with hostile clients.

Chapter Summary

In Chapter 2, focus was on the first skill of cultural diversity competence: understanding culture as multilevel. The culture concept, a conceptual tool for observing and thinking about culture, "the aspects of culture," and each level of culture (personal, subcultural, national, and organizational) were described. Next are opportunities for practice with Worksheets 3 to 10 of Skill One, understanding culture as multilevel. (See Figure 2.1 for a visual representation of Skill One.) In Chapter 3, I will define and provide practice of Skill Two, understanding common barriers to effective relationships.

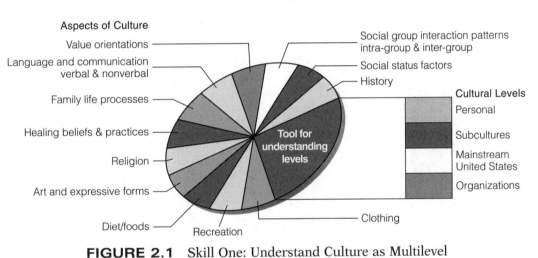

FIGURE 2.1 Skill One: Understand Culture as Multilevel

Worksheet 3

Identifying the Aspects of Culture/Ethnicity (approx. 30–45 minutes)

Purpose: Practice identifying the aspects of culture to increase awareness of the various dimensions of culture.

Instructions:

1. Film analysis (30–45 minutes or longer depending on the length of the film)

   Instructor shows a film about another culture followed by group discussion. Instruct the students/participants to identify as many aspects of culture as they recognized in the film and give an example of each. Use the following worksheet.

   OR

2. Group discussion of aspects of culture (30 minutes)

   Form into small groups. Using the following worksheet, discuss an example of any five aspects of culture that you have observed within the last two days. Assign one group member to write the examples on paper and another to report the examples to the entire group during the whole-group discussion.

Aspects of Culture/Ethnicity

1. History

2. Social Status Factors

3. Social Group Interaction Patterns
   Intragroup relations

   Intergroup relations

4. Value Orientations

5. Language and Communication

   Verbal

   Nonverbal

6. Family Life Processes

7. Healing Beliefs and Practices

8. Religion

9. Art and Expressive Forms

10. Diet/Foods

11. Recreation

12. Clothing

Debriefing Questions

Write the answers to the following questions in the spaces provided.
(approx. 10 minutes)

1. Describe your feelings and thoughts when discussing the five
   aspects identified by your group.

2. What did you learn about yourself in the course of this exercise?

3. What did you learn about others in the course of this exercise?

4. Name two ways you can use what you've learned in your daily life.

Worksheet 4

Experiencing Personal Culture, Part 1

(approx. 20 minutes)

Purpose: To provide an experience of one's personal culture.

Instructions: Think about the following question for 2 or 3 minutes: What is important to me in my daily life? Draw the images or ideas that come into your mind in the following space. Do not write words about your personal culture; draw only stick figures, cartoons, or any other symbols that represent what is important to you.

Debriefing Questions

Write your answers to the following questions. (approx. 10 minutes)

1. Describe your feelings and thoughts as you attempted to portray your perception of your personal culture.

2. What did you learn about yourself in the course of this exercise?

3. What did you learn about others in the course of this exercise?

4. Name two ways in which you can use what you have learned in daily life.

Worksheet 5

Identifying the Aspects of Personal Culture, Part 2 (approx. 20 minutes)

Instructions: Choose three aspects of culture from the list included with this worksheet. Apply your choices to your personal culture. Write an explanation of how each aspect is realized in your daily life.

Example:

Examples of two aspects of my personal culture are family life process and values. I live with my extended family, which is a source of both support and strain. My family structure provides me with ongoing support in the form of dense and intimate communication across 11 households. It also provides all members with important, readily available financial and emotional resources. At the same time, however, common knowledge of one another's life challenges can be a source of stress and strain because each person's struggle is, in some way, everyone's. At another cultural level, my life as a member of an extended family runs counter to the norm of our national or mainstream culture. Mainstream U.S. culture promotes nuclear family structure, composed of father, mother, and children in one household, and it espouses the values of self-autonomy and self-reliance, "pull yourself up by your own bootstraps" and "move out at 18," as opposed to my values of lifelong interdependency and mutual support.

Aspects of Culture to Be Applied to One's Personal Culture

1. History

2. Social Status Factors

3. Social Group Interaction Patterns
   Intragroup
   Intergroup

4. Value Orientations

5. Language and Communication

Verbal

Nonverbal

6. Family Life Processes

7. Healing Beliefs and Practices

8. Religion

9. Art and Expressive Forms

10. Diet/Food

11. Recreation

12. Clothes

Debriefing Questions

Write your answers to these debriefing questions.
(approx. 10 minutes)

1. Describe your feelings and thoughts about applying three aspects to your personal culture.

2. What did you learn about yourself in the course of this exercise?

3. What did you learn about others in the course of this exercise?

4. Name two ways in which you can use what you have learned in daily life.

Worksheet 6

Aspects of Culture as Applied to Subculture or Ethnic Group (approx. 20 minutes)

Purpose: To demonstrate subcultural group-level aspects of culture.

Instructions: Choose three aspects of culture from the following list and apply them to a member of a subculture or ethnic group (it can be your own group). Write an example of each aspect.

Example:

History—My family of origin is Irish Catholic on my father's side. His maternal great grandfather and mother immigrated to Illinois from County Kilkinney, Ireland, during the Great Famine of 1846–49. My mother's paternal great grandfather came from County Cork, Ireland. I am commonly reminded of my Irish origins by the stories told at family gatherings.

Aspects of Culture to be Applied to Subculture/Ethnic Group

1. History

2. Social Status

3. Social Group Interaction Patterns
Intragroup
Intergroup

4. Value Orientations

5. Language and Communication
Verbal
Nonverbal

6. Family Life Processes

7. Healing Beliefs and Practices

8. Religion

9. Art and Expressive Forms

10. Diet/Food

11. Recreation

12. Clothes

Debriefing Questions

Write your answers to the following questions. (approx. 10 minutes)

1. Describe your feelings and thoughts as you applied the three aspects to a subculture/ethnic group.

2. What did you learn about yourself in the course of this exercise?

3. What did you learn about others in the course of this exercise?

4. Name two ways in which you can use what you have learned in daily life.

Worksheet 7

Aspects of Culture as Applied to U.S. Mainstream/National Culture, Nonverbal Communication (approx. 20 minutes)

Purpose: To demonstrate a nonverbal aspect of U.S. national culture in relation to time orientation.

Instructions: Read the characteristics of M-time and P-time in Figure 2.2 that follows. M-time is the prevailing time orientation of U.S. national culture (Hall & Hall, 1987). Cite one example of M-time and P-time that you have witnessed in your daily life and write your answer in the space that follows the figure.

Monochronic or M-Time	Polychronic or P-Time
Schedules and deadlines are very important. There is an urgency to maintain schedules.	Schedules are a goal, but personal commitments are more important and can disrupt one's schedule.
It is important to follow the plan, which is "set in stone."	Plans are flexible, perceived as guidelines, and subject to change.
Promptness, being on time, is a serious activity.	Promptness is a goal, but personal commitments are more important, except in emergencies.
Do one activity at a time; concentrate on the job with no interruptions.	Do several activities at one time; jobs entail multiple tasks, many interruptions.
Rely on direct verbal communication (low context; situational factors not perceived as important for communicating meaning).	Rely on verbal and nonverbal communication (high context; status and other situational factors communicate meaning).
Commitment to job is highly valued.	Commitment to relationships is more important than one's job.
Private property is greatly valued (may be reluctant to lend or borrow).	Private property is not valued over relationships; property is often lent, given away, and borrowed.
Consideration for one's and others' privacy is important.	Continuous and close interactions with family and friends are more important than privacy.
Casual, short-term relationships are acceptable.	Casual, short-term relationships are perceived as superficial.

FIGURE 2.2 Culture as Multilevel: Monochronic and Polychronic Time

Example:

M-time orientation operates in most institutions of the United States, such as the education system with the use of a bell system to stop and start classes.

Debriefing Questions

Write your answers to the debriefing questions. (approx. 10 minutes)

1. Describe your feelings and thoughts as you identified examples of M-time and P-time in your daily life.

2. What did you learn about yourself in the course of this exercise?

3. What did you learn about others in the course of this exercise?

4. Name two ways in which you can use what you have learned in daily life.

Worksheet 8

Aspects of Culture as Applied to U.S. Mainstream/National Culture, Part 2

(approx. 20 minutes)

Purpose: To demonstrate aspects of mainstream U.S. culture.

Instructions: Form groups of four to five people. Discuss any three of the aspects of culture as they relate to mainstream national culture. For each aspect you select, write an example of how it is realized in life, as you have experienced it. If you are taking the class via the Internet (online), identify and write the three aspects of mainstream culture individually. (See "Aspects of U.S. Mainstream/National Culture" in the Appendix for additional information.)

Aspects of Culture to Be Applied to U.S. Mainstream/National Culture

1. History

2. Social Status Factors

3. Social Group Interaction Patterns
   Intragroup
   Intergroup

4. Value Orientations

5. Language and Communication
   Verbal
   Nonverbal

6. Family Life Processes

7. Healing Beliefs and Practices

8. Religion

9. Art and Expressive Forms

10. Diet/Food

11. Recreation

12. Clothes

Debriefing Questions

Write your answers to the debriefing questions. (approx. 10 minutes)

1. Describe your feelings and thoughts as you applied the three aspects to your experience of mainstream/national U.S. culture.

2. What did you learn about yourself in the course of this exercise?

3. What did you learn about others in the course of this exercise?

4. Name two ways in which you can use what you have learned in daily life.

Worksheet 9

Aspects of Organizational Culture and U.S. National Culture (approx. 20 minutes)

Purpose: To demonstrate aspects of organizational culture and its congruence with U.S. national culture.

Instructions: Form into small groups of four to five people. Discuss any three aspects of culture from the following list that characterizes an organization in which you or someone else works. Examine how the aspects relate to U.S. national culture, such as the prevailing use of the M-time system examined in Worksheet 7. If you are taking the class via the Internet (online), identify and write the three aspects of organization culture individually.

Example:

The social status factors in the hospital in which Mary Mercedes works as a nurse reflect the gender stratification that exists in the society at large. The top administrators are primarily white males, and middle and lower management is primarily composed of women (and persons of color and of diverse cultures).

Aspects of Culture as Applied to Organizational Culture

1. History

2. Social Status Factors

3. Social Group Interaction Patterns
   Intragroup

   Intergroup

4. Value Orientations

5. Language and Communication

Verbal

Nonverbal

6. Family Life Processes

7. Healing Beliefs and Practices

8. Religion

9. Art and Expressive Forms

10. Diet/Food

11. Recreation

12. Clothes

Debriefing Questions

Write your answers to the debriefing questions. (approx. 10 minutes)

1. Describe your personal reaction (feelings, thoughts) to applying the three aspects to your experience of organizational culture in the United States.

2. What did you learn about yourself in the course of this exercise?

3. What did you learn about others in the course of this exercise?

4. Name two ways in which you can use what you have learned in daily life.

Worksheet 10

Recognizing the Need to Understand the Aspects of Culture/Ethnicity in an Organization (approx. 30 minutes)

Purpose: To demonstrate the need for cultural understanding in daily life (at work, school, community, family, etc).

Instructions: Form into small groups of four to five persons or do this individually if you are taking the course via the Internet. First, in the space provided below, identify three aspects of culture you need to understand to work or communicate more effectively with colleagues (fellow employees, students, family members, etc.). Second, discuss and identify three aspects of culture you need to understand to work or communicate more effectively with people for whom you are in some way responsible—clients, students, your children. This group also includes those to whom you deliver services or goods.

Example:

1. Aspects of colleagues' culture. Three aspects of culture identified by a group of 35 social service employees as important for understanding their colleagues' cultures were language (both verbal and nonverbal, said it was "basic"), values, and religion. Anther group of 25 nurses in a community hospital also identified language and communication (verbal and nonverbal), values, and religion, yet added family life processes. The nurses said it was essential they understand as much as they can about the family's values, beliefs, and practices to improve their attempts at working together to provide patient-centered health care.

2. Aspects of clients, students, patients, and cultures. Seven aspects of culture were identified by the 35 social service employees as necessary for providing client-centered services: language and communication (verbal and nonverbal), values, religion, family life processes, healing beliefs and practices, diet/foods, and recreation. The 25 nurses cited the same seven and yet added the aspect of social group interaction patterns—both intragroup and intergroup. The nurses said understanding the social group interaction patterns of their patients helps them understand community relations that affect health care in the hospital (intergroup conflict is reflected in the high number of cases in Emergency Care).

Your Example:

1. Three aspects of your colleagues' culture (that is, identify three aspects of culture you need to understand to work with them more congenially and productively). State the reason for your choices.

   Aspect # 1

   Aspect # 2

   Aspect # 3

2. Three aspects of culture of your clients, students, or others for whom you are responsible. State the reason for your choices.

   Aspect # 1

   Aspect # 2

   Aspect # 3

Debriefing Questions

Write your answers to the following questions.

1. Describe your feelings and thoughts as you discussed the aspects in relation to colleagues and clients (patients, students, customers, etc.).

2. What did you learn about yourself in the course of this exercise?

3. What did you learn about others in the course of this exercise?

4. Name two ways in which you can use what you have learned in daily life.

Chapter 3

Skill Two

Understanding the Six Barriers

Understanding Barriers to Effective Relationships

Similar to Skill One, Skill Two fosters cultural awareness and understanding in relation to the aspect of culture, social group interaction patterns. Skills One and Two collectively are referred to as *culture-mindedness*. People who possess culture-mindedness are demonstrating Skills One and Two by attuning to the texture of relationships and by learning about and recognizing different ways of thinking and communicating, and the other aspects of culture, as well as the critical barriers common in social group interaction patterns. Culture-minded people in any given situation attend to the demeanor and behavior of the people with whom they interact. On another level, they are sensitive to the type of relations influenced by the organization's structure and relational processes, the organization's "climate." A culturally competent organization is the result of numerous activities aimed at building a community atmosphere (climate) based on respect, inclusiveness, and support of all employees (Daniels et al., 2001, pp. 51–76).

As Skill One focuses on cultural dimensions—that is, the 12 general aspects of culture and the four levels of culture in which these aspects manifest, the personal, ethnic or subculture group, U.S. mainstream/national, and organizational—Skill Two focuses on six barriers to effective communication and relationships (Pederson, 1988). A list of these six barriers, which focus on the aspect of culture, social group interaction patterns, provides a conceptual tool for recognizing and understanding cultural dynamics at play in group patterns of social interaction, especially when cultural competence is absent and conflict occurs. The six barriers divide conveniently into two broad types based on levels of complexity: the personal/interpersonal level and the organization/systems level.

1). Personal/Interpersonal Barriers
   1. Language (verbal communication)
   2. Nonverbal communication
   3. Preconceptions, stereotypes, and discrimination
   4. Judgments
   5. Stress

2). Organizational/Institutional Barriers
   6. Norms, policies, procedures, and programs unfriendly to cultural diversity

Personal/Interpersonal Barriers

Language refers to the system of verbal communication that was defined previously in the general aspects of culture. The following example illustrates this barrier: Monolingual, Spanish-speaking Mrs. Martinez, seeking an injection for arthritis, becomes highly frustrated when she visits the local monolingual English-speaking clinic. Similarly, *nonverbal communication*—including body stance, body smell, gestures, and eye contact, as defined previously in the general aspects of culture—also can become a barrier to interpersonal relationships. For example, after unsuccessful efforts of the human relations manager to convince a coworker to wear deodorant, other employees refuse to attend meetings in which the offending worker is present, which results in unmet group deadlines.

Preconceptions and stereotypes function as negative lenses through which people perceive others who look and act differently. Such preconceptions and stereotypes are usually based on overgeneralized beliefs, assumptions, and misinformation. For example, Helen, a snowy-haired Euro-American woman is waiting for her flight when she is approached by a patronizing flight representative who asks solicitously, "Would you like wheelchair assistance while boarding?" Angrily, Helen retorts, "Not today, dearie!"

Discriminatory treatment is a natural consequence of the distorted view that results from preconceived and stereotypical thinking. Negative assumptions and beliefs provide psychological permission to behave in ways that discriminate against difference. The following examples illustrate the point: Robert, an African American man, leaves his workplace to deposit his cashed paycheck in a nearby bank. He is detained by a police officer on the suspicion of theft (Meeks, 2000). Gus Jones's application for an apartment is declined by the apartment manager because of the manager's perception of Gus as gay.

Discrimination and prevailing stereotypes center on what some researchers refer to as "isms": racism, sexism, classism, ageism, ableism, and heterosexism (Calasanti & Slevin, 2001; Delgado & Stefancic, 1997; Essed, 1991; Ewen, 1998; Fine et al., 1997; Koppelman, 2005; Sleeter & McLaren, 1995; Stewart & Bennet, 1991; Tatum, 1993, 1997). The isms operate on personal, interpersonal, and institutional levels.

Judgment barriers relate to preconceptions, stereotypes, and discrimination. This barrier is an unconscious and automatic tendency to pass negative judgment on people who look and behave in unfamiliar ways. For example, Mary Johnson, a social worker for 12 years, feels self-righteously justified in correcting the accented speech patterns of her new Vietnamese supervisor, who speaks English as a second language. The negative judgment may derive from *ethnocentrism*, a common human tendency to judge others by one's own cultural values and standards, which are perceived as superior (Ferraro, 1990; Fine et al., 1997; Lett, 1987; Winkelman, 2005). Although equality and social justice are foundation principles of our national/mainstream culture, the traditions of intolerance for diversity, such as nativism and systemic or institutionalized oppression, function as organizational/institutional barriers alongside the foundation principles.

Stress arises as the product of situations in which familiar communication and behavioral cues are missing. This is the fifth personal/interpersonal barrier, referred to as the *stress barrier* (Brislen, 1986; Hall & Hall, 1987; Sikkema & Niyekawa, 1987). This barrier frequently affects all parties. For those treated as minorities in relation to power, opportunities, and respect—namely African Americans, Asians, Latinos, women, elderly, children, GLBTs (gay/lesbian/bisexual/transgender), and persons with disabilities—stress stems from being treated as an "open person," or one who becomes a special target of hostile treatment because she/he is perceived as different and therefore deserving of contempt (Feagin, 1999).

It is useful to think of stress as layered. General stress is experienced by most people in relation to health, family, work, school, and finances. But people of minority status suffer additional stressors such as invisibility. "Invisible" people find themselves routinely ignored or see that their contributions to group efforts at home, school, or work go unacknowledged. Another added stressor is social exclusion, exemplified by the attempt to legally exclude gays from the Boy Scouts of America. Unrelenting pressure to prove oneself, denial of one's personal experience, and verbal and physical harassment or assault all fit in the category of additional stress barriers that minorities must face daily. Moreover, immigrants commonly experience the stress of culture shock when the cues and the fabric of daily life drastically change for them (Foner et al., 2000; Foner & Fredrickson, 2004). The pressure to "hurry up" and learn the language, values, and life patterns of mainstream culture becomes enormous. This pressure is called *acculturation stress* (Padilla, 1986).

Organizational/Institutional Barriers

The second category of barriers to effective communication and relationships is organizational/institutional barriers. Organizational/institutional norms, policies, procedures, and programs set the context for employee relations; when they support disrespectful, unequal, and inequitable relationships among employees, they effectively become the sixth barrier. Cultural assumptions embedded in organizational procedures, processes, and programs are oftentimes highly congruent with the assumptions of mainstream culture (Fine et al., 1997; Hamada & Sibley, 1994; Koppelman, 2005; Schwartzman, 1993; Walck & Jordan, 1995; Wright, 1994).

Five Gender Issues

Five gender issues consistently reported at work sites include:

1. the nonrecognition of women's authority and the unrealistic expectations, based on historical stereotypes, of women's capabilities
2. unequal opportunities, pay, and benefits for women
3. inappropriate sexual behavior directed at women
4. confusion regarding gender-role etiquette and language
5. special difficulty in balancing work and home life

Women promoted to authority positions commonly report that fellow employees, male and female alike, regularly fail to recognize their capabilities and often assume they are unable to meet the demands of their position, especially when the tasks involved have been traditionally defined as "male" tasks. An example is when technical abilities, such as computer or mechanical skills of any sort, are required. With fellow employees assuming their need for help or their inability to do the job, women in such positions often encounter difficulties in asserting their administrative or managerial authority (Estrich, 2000; Featherstone, 2004; Hart & Dalke, 1983; Kanter, 1977; Koppelman, 2005; Powell, 1988, 1994).

Women still experience second-class status in opportunities for promotion, pay, and benefits. The glass ceiling, in other words, remains intact (Estrich, 2000; Ehrenreich & Hochschild, 2002; Featherstone, 2004; Koppelman, 2005).

Women are routinely subjected to inappropriate sexual behavior in the workplace. The emergence of mandatory sexual-harassment training programs amply illustrates the prevalence of inappropriate sexual behavior in the workplace (McCann & McGinn, 1992).

As a result of the economic shift from an industrial-based economy to one of service and information, the majority of American women have been in the workforce since the mid-1970s. This important shift has generated change on several levels. On the family level, a high divorce rate combined with the fact that both men and women function as breadwinners contributes to more women in the workplace. This constitutes gender-role changes and identity changes for women and men because women work in the paid labor force and in the home raising their families as well (Coontz, 1992; Ehrenreich, 1983, 1990, 1991; Eisler, 2002; Hite, 1995; Hochschild, 1997, 2003; Susser & Patterson, 2001). In addition, the far-reaching sociocultural and economic shifts often cause men and women to experience confusion in the workplace regarding gender-role etiquette and expectations: Who pays the tab for the business lunch? Who opens the door for whom? Who calls whom on the phone? Who initiates a romantic encounter? Regarding language, what are the appropriate labels, or forms of address: "Mrs?" "Ms?" "Girl?" "Honey?" "Little Darling?" (Estrich, 2000; Tannen, 1990). Along these same lines, men and women regularly comment on the strain of trying to balance their work and home life (Ehrenreich, 1991; Estrich, 2000; Hochschild, 1997, 2003).

Five Assumptions of U.S. National Culture about Diversity

Five significant assumptions of mainstream culture foster cultural-diversity barriers (Kohls, 1984; Tatum, 1993):

1. The United States is a meritocracy of equal individuals.
2. Americans don't have a culture.
3. If it is different, it is wrong.
4. One should never talk about cultural diversity.
5. One should never admit to being prejudiced.

The United States is a meritocracy. We have all become acquainted with this assumption during our own socialization process in the United States. Schools and the media, two powerful agents of socialization, regularly project U.S. institutions as color-blind and as presenting equal opportunity to all participants. Consequently, because our social system is assumed to be fair, if one does not succeed, he or she is assumed to be at fault because of laziness, negligence, or another personal failure (McIntosh, 1993). When we function under this assumption, an individual's lack of success is never blamed on the society that fails to develop reasonable opportunity structures that are viable for all concerned rather than solely for members of elite groups (Eisenstein, 1994; Sidel, 1978; Susser & Patterson, 2001). It is clear that the national or mainstream culture's core values of individual autonomy and self-determination provide ideological support for the belief in a supposed meritocracy (Fine et al., 1997; Rose, 1990; Stewart & Bennet, 1991).

Americans don't have a culture. This assumption springs from the ideological emphasis on individual autonomy and self-determination prevalent in U.S. society. Supposedly, Americans in the United States don't have a culture because they are autonomous decision makers who create their own individualized way of living (Kohls, 1984). In the operational, day-to-day level, this assumption is experienced as virtually normative and is therefore unconscious and invisible.

If it's different, it's wrong. At times in our history this assumption has been referred to as *racism*. It gives rise to anti-Semitic, antigay, anti-people of color, antiage, anti-Catholic, or any other "anti" sentiment anyone can name. A major support for racist theory is the strong popular belief that different races are distinct biological entities, although science rejects this concept due to the findings that human variation is continuous, not discreet (Kottack & Kozaitis, 2003, pp. 84–120; Lieberman, 1997; Marks, 2005, pp. 1–7; Montagu, 1974). Existing beliefs in the present-day concept of race grew from a European point of view that dates back to at least the early 17th century. As Europeans built their overseas empires in the Americas, Asia, and Africa, their concept of race fostered support for the decimation and impoverishment of the indigenous peoples of these continents. The notion of the inferiority of non-European races burgeoned, becoming culturally constructed in the context of historical events. As it stands today in the United States, the race concept narrowly perceives the entire world being divided into three distinct races: Negroid, Caucasoid, and Asian. These races are described on the basis of such observable physical features as skin color, nasal width, hair texture, and eye shape. The stereotype of "the three big races" has become so prevalent it is viewed "as true, natural and inescapable" (Lieberman, 1997, p. 2; Susser & Patterson, 2001; Winkelman, 2005). This erroneous perception dictates that everyone must belong to one or more of these three races, and that Caucasians/whites are superior. Moreover, in the late 19th century, an additional development in erroneous racial ideology began to overlay the established "big three." European races began to be thought of as composed of only the Nordic, Alpine, and Mediterranean races. The Jews and the Irish were considered separate, "debased" races. Although the biological bases for distinct races has not been scientifically verified, the social reality of race is widely practiced against people of color. Furthermore, it is common for whites in the United States to be unaware of the privilege that accrues to being a member of the perceived white "race" (Delgado & Stefancic, 1997; Wise, 2005).

Another dimension in the development of race ideology of the mainstream culture of the United States is the cultural rule of hypodescent.

The rule of hypodescent, or the "one-drop rule," defines a person as lower in status or position if that person has just one ancestor who was a member of a lower group of that society's group hierarchy. Thus, any person with an African American, Mexican American, or American Indian ancestor is socially defined and perceived as African American, Mexican American, or American Indian, even though that person may identify with his or her Euro-American family of origin. This is how white slave owners increased their slave population before the Civil War. As slave owners fathered babies with black slaves, their wealth grew exponentially because those babies were considered black—and thus slaves. Hypodescent in the United States is quite distinct from its manifestations in other cultures. In Japan, for example, hypodescent is less precise than in the United States, where mixed offspring automatically become members of the minority group. Children of mixed marriages in Japan are stigmatized for their non-Japanese ancestry (Kottack & Kozaitis, 2003, pp. 92–103).

One should never talk about diversity. This widely held assumption is actually a subtle behavioral assumption enforced by the tacit belief in the national policy of "Anglo-conformity" and white supremacy. For decades the Anglo-conformity/white supremacy mentality has worked to implement the forced assimilation of culturally diverse groups. American Indians, during the centuries that European Americans appropriated their lands, and African slaves, before and after the Civil War, serve as two clear examples (Ewen, 1998; Feagin, 1999; Glenn, 2002).

One should never admit to being prejudiced. This final cultural assumption on our list is also age-old and equally tacit. Never admitting personal prejudice is a dynamic that works to curtail even the perception, let alone the discussion and analysis, of institutional and systemic inequities, thus supporting the belief in meritocracy.

Chapter Summary

In Chapter 3 we have considered the six barriers to effective relationships that occur in social group interaction patterns, an aspect of culture described in Chapter 2. Cultural-mindedness is achieved when Skills One and Two are understood. Thus, understanding the aspects of culture as they operate on the personal, subcultural, national, and organization levels (Skill One) is just one part of cultural-mindedness. Skill Two, understanding the six barriers that can manifest in social group interaction patterns, is also essential for achieving cultural-mindedness. See a visual representation of Skill Two in Figure 3.1 below. In Chapter 4 we will turn our attention to culturally centered communication skills.

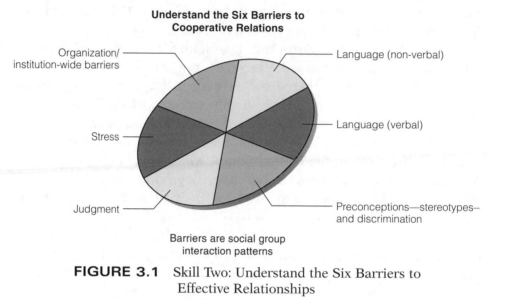

FIGURE 3.1   Skill Two: Understand the Six Barriers to Effective Relationships

Worksheet 11

Barriers to Communication: Cross-Cultural Speaking (approx. 30 minutes)

Purpose: To foster awareness and understanding of the verbal and nonverbal barriers to communication in a culturally diverse context.

Instructions: Form four groups, named 1, 2, 3, and 4. Your instructor will hand your group a set of instructions (the four cultural scripts are in the Instructor's Manual). Then pair off with someone from another group and, following your instructions, learn three points of information about the other person through simple chatting.

Debriefing Questions

Write your answers to the debriefing questions.

1. Describe your personal reaction (feelings, thoughts) to the role-playing exercise as applied to the verbal and nonverbal barriers to effective communication and relationships that can arise in a culturally diverse context. Did you experience any of the other barriers?

2. Ask one person from each of the four groups to read his or her script aloud before the whole group.

3. What did you learn about yourself in the course of this exercise?

4. What did you learn about others in the course of this exercise?

5. Name two ways in which you can use what you have learned in daily life.

Worksheet 12

Barriers to Effective Relationships: Case of the Green-Haired People (approx. 30 minutes)

Purpose: To foster awareness and understanding of the six barriers to effective communication and relationships in culturally diverse settings.

Instructions: Read the following scenario, "The Case of the People with Green Hair."

The Case of the People with Green Hair

John Doe is not born with prejudice against other human beings who have green hair. But from the time he is a tiny tot, John Doe is warned against them. Don't play with the children with green hair. Don't talk to them. Stay with your own kind. You're a bad boy, John Doe, if you have anything to do with the green-haired children. John Doe learns not only from his parents' words but also from tone of voice, facial expressions, and gestures.

As John grows older, he learns that his parents and their friends and neighbors do not want people with green hair to attend his church, to live in his neighborhood, to go to his school, or playground, or camp. The adults who control John's life, and whom he imitates and depends on, insist that the people with green hair stay in their place. Everybody with whom little John Doe is acquainted believes that green-haired people should worship elsewhere, live elsewhere, and be educated elsewhere. As a child, John Doe very seldom even sees people with green hair.

As to jobs, the family of little John Doe believes that people with green hair should do the heavy and the dirty work that people like John Doe's folks need done but don't want to do themselves. The better jobs, in professions or businesses, should belong to people like John's father and mother. If people with green hair do hold any such job, they should be restricted to working for their own kind, the people with green hair.

The people with green hair whom John does encounter are those who do the heavy and the dirty jobs for his family. Naturally, these folks do not happen to be the more able green-haired people. Instead, they are the people who can obtain only this type of work. They are not well educated. They dress poorly. They get dirty on the job. So John Doe's first actual childhood experiences with the people with green hair help persuade him that his family is right.

Green-haired people, he can plainly see, are inferior people. They are perceived as uneducated, poor, dirty.

The way things are, there can be almost no communication between John Doe and the people with green hair. John has no reliable way of telling what green-haired people are thinking. True, he occasionally reads about people with green hair in his local newspaper. But, since conflict makes news, his newspaper usually reports on people with green hair who happen to get themselves into trouble with the law. When the name of a person with green hair appears in the news, the local newspaper carefully places the words "green hair" after the individual's name. John often comes away from his newspaper with the clear impression that too many green-haired people get themselves into difficult situations. The conclusion that everything has conspired to teach him since infancy becomes more confirmed. People with green hair are people who do bad things. Even the newspapers say so.

Since he has no way of communicating directly with people who have green hair, John Doe is an easy prey for wild rumors concerning "greenies," as many contemptuously call them. John hears that "greenies" want to marry people with "superior" hair color and thus make everybody's hair partly green. Though people with green hair repeatedly deny this rumor and plaintively explain that all they want is to be treated like human beings, John clutches on to the rumor. It strengthens his resolve to keep people with green hair in their place so that people like himself and his family will not be forced to live at the low level at which the people with green hair are forced to live.

Time moves along. John Doe becomes a man. He follows the patterns he has learned. He marries Jane Doe, who has learned the same prejudices against people with green hair. Eventually, they become parents. And what do they teach their children? "Don't play with the children with green hair. You are bad if you do."

John Doe has learned to be prejudiced against people with green hair. How did John get that way? The total environment in which John Doe lived encouraged prejudice against people with green hair. He learned his prejudices from his parents, their friends, and his neighbors. He learned them from his limited observations. He learned them from his reading of his newspaper. He learned them from his separation from green-haired people on his job. He developed an unattractive picture in his mind, an ugly stereotype of people with green hair. So, in turn, John Doe carried over his prejudices to his children. Because they noticed and imitated their father's feelings, John Doe's children, too, became infected with the disease called prejudice.

Nothing ever broke the circle that closed John Doe in with his prejudices against people with green hair. Things were so arranged by John Doe's family that he found himself walled in by the circle almost from birth. In turn, John Doe began to build a circle of prejudice around his own children from the time of their birth.

Debriefing Questions

Write your answers to the debriefing questions.

1. Describe your personal reaction (feelings, thoughts) to reading and discussing the case example.

2. How many barriers are evident in the case of the green-haired people?

3. What did you learn about yourself in the course of this exercise?

4. What did you learn about others in the course of this exercise?

5. Name two ways in which you can use what you have learned in daily life.

Worksheet 13

Barriers to Effective Relationships: Case Analysis, Part 1, Personal/ Interpersonal Level (approx. 30 minutes)

Purpose: To foster awareness and understanding of the personal and interpersonal barriers to communication and congenial relationships in culturally diverse contexts.

Instructions:

1. Form into small groups of four to five people (or do the activity individually if you are in an Internet course) and describe in the space that follows a cultural diversity issue or conflict occurring in any setting within the last year. It might be an incident you experienced personally or one you heard about. Try to be alert to the national culture's five assumptions about diversity that were previously discussed ("Americans don't have a culture," "if it is different it is wrong," "the U.S. is a meritocracy," "never talk about diversity," "never admit to prejudice"). Try also to include such elements of diversity as gender, ethnicity, race, age, disability, socioeconomic status, sexual orientation, religion, and verbal and nonverbal communication. Feel free to frame your discussion from any number of points of view and roles: as a supervisor or subordinate in a supervisory relationship, for example; as a teacher or student in a teacher-student relationship; or as a coworker in a work situation. Discuss and identify the operative barriers.

Example:

I was employed as an attorney at a law firm, and one of my duties was to conduct initial interviews of prospective clients to determine if they had a viable case. A Chinese man was ushered into my office, and I introduced myself as the attorney who would be interviewing him. He stopped dead and expressed great surprise and consternation at being interviewed by a woman. He said he had expected to see a man and asked if there was a man available. I told him I was the only person there but I could direct him to another office if he felt uncomfortable talking to me. He said he needed to think about it so I explained my background to him while he was pondering. He finally agreed to stay and suddenly turned very respectful. He insisted on calling me "Doctor" even after I explained to him that attorneys are not usually called Doctor.

The barriers in this case include preconceptions and stereotyping relative to gender in his assumption that only men are attorneys;

judgment and discrimination would also apply if he had requested a male attorney to replace the female attorney as he seemed to contemplate for a moment.

Write your Case Example here:

Write the barriers identified in the case here:

Debriefing Questions

Write your answers to the following debriefing questions.

1. Describe your personal reaction (feelings, thoughts) to the foregoing exercise.

2. What did you learn about yourself in the course of this exercise?

3. What did you learn about others in the course of this exercise?

4. Name two ways in which you can use what you have learned in daily life.

Worksheet 14

Barriers to Effective Relationships: Case Analysis, Part 2, Organization-Wide Level (approx. 30 minutes)

Purpose: To foster awareness and understanding of organizational and institutional barriers to effective communication and relationships in culturally diverse contexts.

Instructions: Form into small groups of four to five people (or do the activity individually if you are in an Internet course) and describe in the space that follows a cultural diversity issue or conflict occurring in a work or community setting within the last year that suggests a barrier in the policy toward diversity. It might be an incident you experienced personally or one you heard about. It may include such elements of diversity as gender, ethnicity, race, age, disability, religion, socioeconomic status, and sexual orientation. Feel free to frame your discussion from any number of points of view and roles: as a supervisor or subordinate in a supervisory relationship, for example; as a teacher or student in a teacher-student relationship; or as a coworker in a work situation. Discuss the specific barriers you can isolate in the case example you describe; list these barriers and cite specific concrete examples. Then regroup with the class to discuss the case examples and analyses produced in each of the small groups.

Example:

An elementary school in my district has numerous teaching assistants who are all Hispanic. The principal and teachers use and treat them as if they were maids instead of assistants. They talk down to them and order them around. They never sit with them during lunch or socialize with them in the lunchroom or at any of the events during the school year such as Christmas. The teachers cluster in their group and the Hispanic assistants cluster in their group with little or no social communication between groups. The barrier in this case is an organization-wide pattern of practice (policy) of exclusion and disrespect.

Write your Case Example here:

Write the organization-wide barrier here:

Debriefing Questions

Write your answers to the following debriefing questions.

1. Describe your personal reaction (feelings, thoughts) to the foregoing exercise.

2. What did you learn about yourself in the course of this exercise?

3. What did you learn about others in the course of this exercise?

4. Name two ways in which you can use what you have learned in daily life.

Chapter 4

Skill Three

Practicing Culturally Centered Communication Skills

The Personal Competencies

This first part of Chapter 4 sets out a list of 14 personal competencies for establishing effective relationships across cultural differences. I have isolated and refined these competencies from the work of various researchers and practitioners (Hogan-Garcia, 1991, 1995). The competencies are important individually, and they are interrelated as well. Daily practice of these competencies, the daily work of making them your personal culture by applying them first to yourself, builds a personal foundation for engaging in the dialogue and conflict-recovery process in a culturally diverse environment.

The development of the triple skills of dialogue, conflict recovery, and problem solving, all pivotal and essential to one another, provide critical information about the culturally diverse ways people think and behave. In this respect, they make effective interaction possible. Without the reflective practice of the personal competencies as a foundation, the six barriers to effective communication will inevitably arise, and the dialogue process will die, rendering the conflict-recovery and problem-solving processes impossible. Notice how intricately each part of the interpersonal process—dialogue, conflict recovery, and problem solving—hinges on the development of the following 14 personal competencies. In fact, they are so essential I believe it is necessary to frame them as directives.

1. Be nonjudgmental.
2. Be flexible.
3. Be resourceful.
4. Personalize observations.
5. Pay attention to thoughts and feelings.

6. Listen carefully.

7. Observe attentively.

8. Assume complexity.

9. Tolerate the stress of uncertainty.

10. Have patience.

11. Manage personal biases and stereotypes.

12. Keep a sense of humor.

13. Show respect.

14. Show empathy.

This list of cultural competencies can be viewed as the "14 commandments" of the culturally competent person. Let us review each in turn.

1. **Be nonjudgmental.** Short-circuit, unplug, or otherwise disable the common tendency to judge negatively others you perceive as different. Negative judgment casts an unfavorable light on the other person, allowing you to view the other with disfavor. For example, Mary Ryan thinks "vile" thoughts when Joyce Carruthers appears at her office door dressed in shabby clothing with spiked hair, yellow teeth, and foul breath. Mary becomes appalled at the suddenness of her judgmental thoughts when she discovers that Joyce, rather than being the new homeless woman assigned to her already overburdened caseload, is her new coworker and office mate.

2. **Be flexible.** Adjust and readjust, as often as necessary, to quickly changing situations. For example, Mary Ryan rearranges her office furniture nearer the window and confers regularly with her supervisor in an effort to adjust quickly, amicably, and effectively to her new office mate.

3. **Be resourceful.** Obtain the needed information and articles you will need to respond effectively to any given situation. For example, consider the microwave and the workspace. Food odors often offend. One effective response would be to supply a simple fan to circulate and diffuse the air or to call a group meeting to brainstorm solutions. In one case, a supervisor tactfully polled members for solutions to be proposed at the regular office meeting.

4. **Personalize observations.** Express your personal feelings, thoughts, ideas, and beliefs appropriately, warmly or empathetically if the situation warrants, in order to show the other person that you care about him/her *as an individual,* one fellow human being to another. When you practice this particular competency, you show that you recognize that one's personal perceptions, feelings, attitudes, and beliefs may not be shared by the other person.

Three attendant skills, drawn from counseling practice, help personalize observations (Ivey & Gluckstern, 1982; Leviton & Greenstone, 1997).

1. Communicate with "I-messages" rather than "you-messages." For example, "I disagree" is an I-message, not "you're wrong."

2. Paraphrase. Repeat what you hear in conversation back to the other person. For example, "Am I hearing you say that you want to reschedule our meeting?"

3. Listen actively. Active listening entails giving the speaker your undivided attention. Look at the speaker and listen intently. Avoid distractions. Do not begin to think about your response until the speaker is done talking. Use verbal cues such as "uh-huhs" and "yes" to demonstrate that you're listening.

5. **Pay attention to thoughts and feelings.** Take your own thoughts and feelings seriously. Keep in touch with your interior reactions to the people with whom you verbally interact. If you remain alert to your interior responses, you can more easily frame your verbal and nonverbal responses in effective ways. When you pay attention to yourself and your internal responses, you remain in charge of the interpersonal situation. By paying attention to your thoughts and feelings, you put yourself in better charge of yourself and in better command of the interpersonal situation. Mary Ryan, in the previous scenario, serves to exemplify this point. She paid close attention to her own feelings, recognized her tendency to judge negatively, and worked through this to ameliorate the situation in a timely fashion.

6. **and 7. Listen attentively/observe carefully.** These two competencies overlap. Attentive listening and careful observation serve to increase one's sensitivity to the "whole message," not just the words, but the message beyond the words. Pay attention to tone, body posture and stance, gestures, and facial expression. For example, Joe Wong, a business manager, experiences great difficulty understanding his new administrative assistant, Vietnamese American Mary Nguyen. To cope with his frustration, Wong self-consciously listens with added attention and carefully observes Mary's responses during his conversations with her. He frequently assesses his understanding with responses such as "If I understand you correctly . . . ," "Yes, I see . . . ," and "Would you mind repeating. . . ."

8. **Assume complexity.** Recognize in an ongoing way that in a culturally challenging situation, diverse perspectives and outcomes remain multiple in nature. Administrative assistant Mike Rodriguez, a monolingual English speaker, is routinely asked to translate Spanish words and phrases into English for his coworkers throughout the company. They assume, because of his Spanish

surname, that he understands Spanish. Paradoxically, Mary Johnson, fluent in English and Spanish, routinely employs her linguistic skill in assisting bilingual clients but finds herself rebuffed or ignored by them because she has blond hair, blue eyes, and white skin. To native Spanish speakers, she is an outsider.

9. **Tolerate the stress of uncertainty.** Avoid showing irritation or annoyance with the ambiguity of the culturally diverse situation. This overlaps with competency #5. The powerful emotions of fear, anger, anxiety, and frustration, when they present themselves, demand serious attention during culturally diverse encounters. For example, Vietnamese emigrant Ba That, upon arrival at L.A. International Airport, becomes appalled at the spectacle of the people who surround her, hugging and kissing, upon their reunion with family and loved ones. "What are they doing?" she asks, aghast, as she explains to her sponsor that she had never witnessed such personal and physical displays of affection in her native land.

10. **Have patience.** This competence is a positive and effective response to stress. One needs to practice maintaining calm while, at the same time, continuing steadily and persistently through challenging situations. For example, in the lunch line, Mike Rodriguez, a light-skinned, Irish-Mexican American, finds himself the object of an irate Julio Dominguez who repeatedly jabs his arm demanding, "How can you be 'Rodriguez' with white skin like that?" Alarmed at the suddenness of the outburst, Mike maintains his poise and quietly touches Julio's arm, saying: "It's alright, Julio, my mother is Irish." Later that same day, Mike again maintains his patience when he is derisively told by a Euro-American male coworker, "Man, am I sorry for you, having a name like Rodriguez!"

11. **Manage personal biases.** Make the effort to grow beyond your personal viewpoint in order to treat people with whom you interact respectfully, as individuals, and with full acknowledgement that no one person typifies an entire group. For example, Lash is a gay, white, male, trained crisis-line volunteer and receptionist who works at a local gay-lesbian-bi-transgendered (GLBT) service agency. Alone one evening, he finds himself confronted with a flamboyant cross-dressed client, who turns out to be a transgendered person in transition seeking peer counseling regarding an upcoming preliminary sex-change surgery. Lash, recoiling at the client's personal appearance and deeply horrified at the mention of sex-reassignment surgery, nevertheless manages a calm and poised demeanor in the course of his conversation with the client. He diplomatically suggests that the client might be better served by another transgendered

person known to the agency and proceeds to make the necessary recommendation.

12. **Keep a sense of humor.** Cultivate an active awareness of the absurdity that often arises when cultural differences converge. Avoid taking things so seriously that you lose your perspective and are unable to laugh at yourself. Learn to laugh *with* others, never *at* others. Find humor in the irony of life. For example, a manager in an assembly plant with mostly first-generation Vietnamese employees gestured "good luck" to them at the end of team meeting. Later, he was aghast when he learned the gesture was the "dirty finger signal" in their home country. When he heard that many of the Vietnamese American employees realized the mistake and thought the interaction was hilarious, the manager laughed as well, especially as he recalled the surprised looks on many of their faces. To an outsider, there is a somewhat surprising incongruity in the routine intolerance exhibited by one victimized group toward another, or one victimized individual toward another: Latino vs. African American, African American vs. Jewish person, Greek vs. Vietnamese, Irish vs. African American, liberationist woman vs. housewife, flamboyant gay male vs. buttoned-down gay executive, or a grocery store clerk to a dwarf who needs help reaching items on the grocery shelves.

13. **Show respect.** Go out of your way to express genuinely the understanding, honor, and esteem that you continually cultivate for the persons with whom you are interacting. For example, the instructor who carefully avoids words and gestures that might be open to misinterpretation by members of different cultural groups actively remembers that symbols and gestures vary greatly between cultures.

14. **Show empathy.** Experience the other person's perspectives, feelings, beliefs, and attitudes as if they were your own. To use an old cliché, put yourself in the other person's shoes. Empathy is critical in a culturally diverse encounter. One effective and enjoyable stratagem for enlarging empathy is an ongoing reading program focused on "minority" or "special interest" novels. A huge and ever growing library of novels is amassing from the Chicano/Chicana, Latin American, African American, Asian American, feminist, gay and lesbian experiences, and persons with disabilities, to name only a few (Anzaldua, 1990; Bell, 1979; Chan, 1994; Chow, 1998; DuBois & Ruiz, 1990; Eng, 1999; Freeman, 1989; Gil & Vazquez, 1996; Gutmann, 1996; Hogan-Garcia & Wright, 1989; Hooks, 2000, 2003; Kikumura, 1981; Liu, 1998; Mackelprang & Salsgiver, 1999; McKinney, 2005; Shipek, 1991; Ward, 1998; Weatherford, 1991).

The Dialogue Process

Dialogue is the exchange of information between people intent on listening to one another's perspective to comprehend the meaning. It is based on the premise of mutual respect and open inquiry and does not involve proving the rightness of one's viewpoint. The dialogue process proceeds in four steps.

Step One: The parties initiate the dialogue by establishing the ground rules of procedure. They mutually determine what is and what is not allowed. They mutually agree to listen and learn about each other's viewpoint.

Step Two: The parties in dialogue listen without interruption and with undivided attention to the viewpoints of each party.

Step Three: Each party restates what he or she thinks was heard. This step permits the parties to demonstrate that they were listening and to verify what they actually heard. Points of misunderstanding or forgotten points come to the fore at this step, which avoids further conflict and allows the parties to rephrase and refine their comments, observations, and viewpoints.

Step Four: Each party gives voice to his or her viewpoint. This means that the parties give *full* expression to their thoughts and feelings about the subject of dialogue.

Of the four steps, the final is pivotal. In one project, for example, administrators of a school district wanted to improve relations with the parents of the African American students in the district. To further this initiative, they convened a community forum to discuss the parents' issues and concerns. For one hour the hurt and angry parents took turns voicing their thoughts, feelings, and views. At this point in the forum the administrators did not follow up with a statement of their own views, nor did they describe the programs they were formulating to address the parents' concerns and to include the parents in the district's school policies. Having politely listened to the parents, the administrators simply closed the meeting.

With the omission of the pivotal fourth step, no dialogue took place between the African American parents and the school administrators; therefore, no meaningful remedies were negotiated for the frustrated parents. In dialogue, all parties need to participate in the discussion. All parties need to freely, candidly, and honestly share their views. This example shows how the dialogue process fails when all parties do not participate equally. Given the magnitude of the parents' grievances, the administrators needed to give the dialogue process more time, and they should have verbally responded to the parents' grievances. If immediate solutions could not be agreed upon, the administrators should have offered more open dialogue, compromise, and further dialogue sessions as a means of fostering the growth of a close working relationship between administrators and parents.

The Conflict Recovery Process

Awareness and practice of recovery skills are needed for reestablishing rapport when mistakes and conflicts occur. The conflict recovery process, like the dialogue process, proceeds in four steps.

Step One: The parties begin the conflict recovery process by openly acknowledging the point of disagreement, misunderstanding, or hostility. They do this in a proactive manner—that is, with the clear determination to solve the point of difficulty, *not* merely to rehearse grievances, fix blame, or allot punishment.

Step Two: The parties engage in the dialogue process about the issue with the use of the problem-solving process discussed next.

Step Three: The parties discuss whatever options they can devise for reducing conflict and work out a plan of action with designated tasks according to a suitable timetable agreeable to all parties. The problem-solving process discussed next is appropriate for this stage of conflict recovery.

Step Four: The parties agree to work with a mediator or culture broker, if necessary, to explore their dispute more fully and to come to some kind of agreement. Notably, in the case of the administrators vs. the African American parents, I suggested the parties engage a mediator in order to reestablish trust and initiate a new dialogue.

The conflict recovery process envisioned here is a dynamic, ongoing series of initiatives that continually address the sources of conflict in a given group and works to bring about positive change. In this sense, conflict resolution may be an elusive and unrealistic goal, whereas the conflict management and the conflict healing implied in the term *conflict recovery* may provide a more useful model from which to work.

The Problem-Solving Process

The problem-solving process provides opportunities to put the 14 personal competencies, the dialogue process, and the conflict recovery techniques into practice. This process is composed of six steps that, to be effective, need to be approached with flexibility according to one's personal style and the particular circumstances of the problematic situation. In other words, the process needs to be tailored to the specific needs of all individuals involved and to the particular group focus.

1. **Define the problem.** Recognize the problem and define it in terms that reflect everyone's views and in terms that are clear to all. Specifically name the objectionable behaviors and their consequences that make up the problem.

2. **Identify possible solutions and generate a list.** Brainstorm a variety of solutions. Ask questions such as, "What are some possible solutions to this problem?" "How many ideas can we list?" Remember, the object of brainstorming is to generate as many ideas as possible in the time available, regardless of their feasibility. The more ideas the better. All ideas are welcome. We are creating a pool of ideas to draw on, from which we design a practical and effective plan of action.

3. **Evaluate the list of possible solutions.** This step, in which the list of possible solutions is subjected to critical examination and analysis, is actually a process of deliberation and the natural follow-up to the brainstorming process. All participants need to express their ideas and feelings about the list; they need to be clear about which solutions are unacceptable and why. In promoting or rejecting a given solution, for example, the reasons why the solution will or will not work need to be pinpointed for discussion. In this way, positive effects or unforeseen negative effects, why a given solution does not satisfy a particular need or why a given solution seems unfair, will all be clarified.

4. **Choose a proposed solution for implementation.** This step, the end product of Step 3, can only come about through *open* discussion among all the members of the group. A true group choice will gradually emerge.

5. **Devise an implementation plan for the solution.** In this step, the group reflects on how to go about implementing the solution on which participants have agreed. An implementation plan is a blueprint for action, a step-by-step outline for putting the solution into effect. The group discusses the series of actions called for by the solution, determines a concrete sequence of steps, specifies a practical timetable for each step, and designates specific tasks. Flexibility and feasibility become key dynamics in determining timetables and sequencing tasks in each step of the implementation plan. Evaluation tools are vital for monitoring both the progress and effectiveness of the implementation plan. Both formative and summative evaluation measures are useful, if possible. A formative evaluation measures the success of the solution as it unfolds; that is, it shows the progress or lack of progress in resolving the original problem situation. A summative evaluation provides an overall assessment of the implementation plan (Fitz-Gibbon & Morris, 1987).

6. **Assess the success of the solution.** The group establishes a mutually agreeable period for assessing the success of the solution

after its implementation. The objective in this assessment is to see how effective the solution was and to determine how satisfied the parties are with it. Both the formative and summative evaluation measures become useful here. If these measures have been taken in the course of the implementation plan, the group will now have documentation of the history of the process, which will give depth and background to the formative and summative evaluations.

Chapter Summary

In Chapter 4 we have worked with the third skill of cultural diversity competence: the 14 personal competencies and the interpersonal processes of dialogue, conflict recovery, and collaborative problem solving. For visual representation of the personal competencies and the dialog process, see Figures 4.1 and 4.2. In Chapter 5 we will use the first three skills to practice the development of organizational action plans for implementing cultural competence throughout the organization.

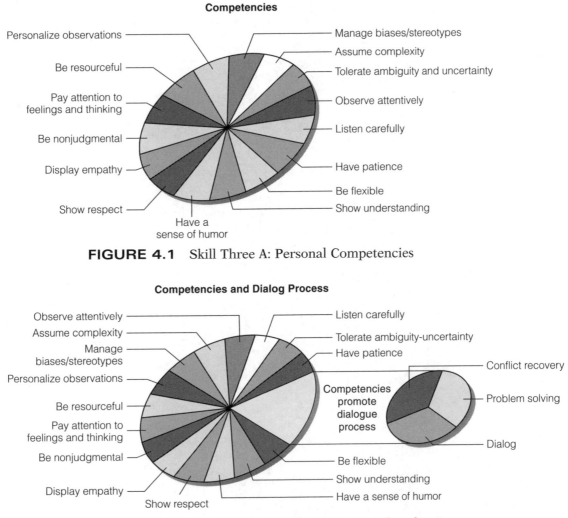

FIGURE 4.1 Skill Three A: Personal Competencies

FIGURE 4.2 Skill Three B: Competencies and Dialog Process

Worksheet 15

Fourteen Personal Competencies Self-Test

(approx. 10 minutes)

Purpose: To foster awareness of the 14 personal competencies through self-assessment.

Instructions: Rate yourself on a scale of 1 (low) to 5 (high) in each of the competencies as defined by the instructor.

1. _____ Be nonjudgmental.

2. _____ Be flexible.

3. _____ Be resourceful.

4. _____ Personalize observations.

5. _____ Pay attention to your thoughts/feelings.

6. _____ Listen carefully.

7. _____ Observe attentively.

8. _____ Assume complexity.

9. _____ Tolerate the stress of uncertainty.

10. _____ Have patience.

11. _____ Manage personal biases and stereotypes.

12. _____ Keep a sense of humor.

13. _____ Show respect.

14. _____ Display empathy.

Evaluating the Score

Add up the points:
61–70 = Highly Competent
51–60 = Moderately Competent
0–50 = Need More Practice

Debriefing Questions

Write your answers to the debriefing questions.

1. Describe your personal reaction (feelings, thoughts) to this self-assessment exercise.

2. What did you learn about yourself in the course of this exercise?

3. What did you learn about others in the course of this exercise?

4. Name two ways in which you can use what you have learned in daily life.

Worksheet 16

Two Communication Skills for Effective Dialogue (approx. 30 minutes)

Purpose: To practice two communication skills that help integrate personal competencies into dialogues.

Instructions:

1. **I-message vs. you-message.** Pair off with someone next to you. Devise a conversational scenario in which two people are talking. Then let each person take turns performing the scenario, employing first the you-message format and second the I-message format.

   Example:

   Two colleagues are discussing directions to a meeting in another building. One colleague, visibly angry, yells: "YOU'RE WRONG!" (you-message). The other colleague replies: "I disagree. I think it's this way" (I-message).

2. **Paraphrasing.** Pair off with someone next to you for each of the interactions. Next, discuss and paraphrase a response for each of the following scenarios. Paraphasing is an important skill in the dialogue process, and may require practice. After the pairs practice a paraphrase response, role play the response to the whole group (if time permits, I ask one member in each pair to read the original statement and the other person in each pair to paraphrase the statement).

   1. "I had a dream last night. I dreamed the grandchildren came over to visit their old granddad. But that's dreams for you. Nobody comes over to see me anymore."

   2. "If you take a job, it'll just ruin our marriage. There's no way I'm going to start washing the dishes and cooking food—that's your job!"

   3. "Why should I clean up my room? It's *mine,* and I'm perfectly comfortable with it. You're just too picky."

   4. "How could you even think of taking a job when your child is so young?"

   5. "I've worked in this department for 10 years, and now my new manager comes in and never listens to me. He acts as if he knows everything, but the department's workload is more and more behind. Oh, what's the use?"

Debriefing Questions

Write your answers to the debriefing questions in the following spaces.

1. Describe your personal reaction (feelings, thoughts) to the communication exercise.

2. What did you learn about yourself in the course of this exercise?

3. What did you learn about others in the course of this exercise?

4. Name two ways in which you can use what you have learned in daily life.

Worksheet 17

Personal Competencies and Your Work Setting (approx. 15 minutes)

Purpose: To foster awareness and understanding of the 14 personal competencies for maintaining effective communication and relationships in a culturally diverse work setting and to practice the dialogue process.

Instructions: Form groups of four or five people. Discuss and identify three competencies important for effective relations with coworkers and clients (or patients, students—those to whom service or a product is provided). The result of your discussion will be two lists of three competencies each to be shared in the whole-group discussion. If you are in an Internet course, do this worksheet individually.

1. Three competencies to be used with coworkers:

2. Three competencies to be used with clients (or patients, students, customers, community at large):

Debriefing Questions

Write your answers to the debriefing questions.

1. Describe your personal reaction (feelings, thoughts) to the exercise as applied to the cultural competencies that ensure effective communication and relationships amidst cultural diversity.

2. What did you learn about yourself in the course of this exercise?

3. What did you learn about others in the course of this exercise?

4. Name two ways in which you can use what you have learned in daily life.

Worksheet 18

The 14 Personal Competencies Case Analysis (approx. 25 minutes)

Purpose: To foster awareness and understanding of the 14 personal competencies for maintaining effective communication and relationships in a culturally diverse context and to practice the dialogue process.

Instructions: Form groups of four or five people. Using the two case examples you developed in Worksheets 13 and 14, discuss and identify any competencies that would *improve* the interaction in the case examples. In conclusion, present your analysis to the class.

Case 1 competencies:

Case 2 competencies:

Debriefing Questions

Write your answers to the debriefing questions.

1. Describe your personal reaction (feelings, thoughts) to the exercise as applied to the cultural competencies that ensure effective communication and relationships amidst cultural diversity.

2. What did you learn about yourself in the course of this exercise?

3. What did you learn about others in the course of this exercise?

4. Name two ways in which you can use what you have learned in daily life.

Worksheet 19

Using Dialogue in Case Analysis

(approx. 45 minutes)

Purpose: To practice the first three skills of cultural competence (from Chapters 2, 3, and 4).

Instructions: Form groups of four or five people. Select and discuss three case examples of a diversity issue from the list below. If you are taking this course online, post your discussion of the cases on the course Discussion Board. For each case, engage in a dialogue in relation to these questions:

1. What aspects and levels of culture do you see in each case (Skill One)?

2. What barriers do you see operating in each case (Skill Two)?

3. What competencies would improve the interactions in each case (Skill Three)?

Let someone in the group write down the group's answers to the questions on a separate sheet and someone else serve as spokesperson for the group in the whole-class discussion.

Case Examples:

1. Business office. People from different cultures are taught to respect authority. You call a "team" meeting, with a desire for serious input, ideas, and feedback—even disagreement, if that's what it takes to find solutions and resolve issues. The cultural background of the team members, however, appears to hinder them in questioning or disagreeing with what they perceive as authority. How can this be resolved?

2. County government office. An employee from Central America refuses to follow orders from shift leads. This employee is male and the shift leads are females. He does, however, accept my orders as the unit supervisor, although I also am female. It seems that three female bosses are too much for him. Where do we go with this?

3. Factory. In dealing with diverse cultural groups, I do not permit or condone ethnic jokes in the working environment, but one cultural group repeatedly engages in this behavior targeting their own ethnic group. The jokes and comments are in fact degrading and demeaning. They are also counterproductive for the promotion of respect for differing cultures. The "group" thinks, however, that because the jokes target themselves, they are okay. What approaches are called for in resolving this issue?

4. **School district office.** A job task requires three Latino professionals to work together as a team. One is Mexican American, one Salvadoran, and the third Puerto Rican. Each speaks Spanish as well as English. There is a great deal of animosity among the members of this group. One member says another acts "bossy" and "aristocratic" and treats others as "servants." Another complains that one member is always "rude." The conflicts seem to relate to cultural and social-status issues. How might conflict here be addressed more effectively?

5. **Hospital care facility.** Early this afternoon Mrs. Vahahrami, an East Indian in her mid-20s, has given birth to a healthy baby boy. Following the birth of the boy, Mr. Vahahrami and his mother have come to see the patient. In accordance with hospital procedure, the delivering doctor, Dr. Garibaldi, has the baby dressed in hospital clothing and sent to the nursery for the night while the mother recuperates. During the labor and birthing procedures, it is necessary to draw some of Mrs. Vahahrami's blood. These procedures are met with harsh glares and a rise in tension between the patient and family and the delivering doctor.

   As another precaution, Dr. Garibaldi reminds Mr. and Mrs. Vahahrami that they are to abstain from sex for six weeks, and he recommends routine circumcision for the new infant. Mrs. Vahahrami, Mr. Vahahrami, and Mr. Vahahrami's mother all look extremely shocked and revolted at these recommendations, and Mrs. Vahahrami begins to weep. Throughout the day, tension between the delivering doctor and the patient and family slowly rises, culminating in Mrs. Vahahrami's crying episode. The family, moreover, has shown reluctance to adhere to some of the doctor's requests; in particular, Mr. Vahahrami has voiced adamant refusal to have his son circumcised, which he considers unwarranted genital mutilation.

   Dr. Garibaldi is greatly confused by the agitated behavior of his patient and her family and has decided that this problem has become too great and must be resolved. What directions might he and his staff take? (written by Craig Goralski)

6. **Grocery store.** A customer was speaking loudly and was pointing her finger at the developmentally delayed adult grocery store bagger. The customer belittled the bagger for "improperly bagging" her groceries as she directed her comments to the cashier. The customer, whose tone of voice was now yelling, said the market should "never hire inept people like that." The bagger looked down and did not make eye contact with anyone. The cashier put her hand on the bagger's arm, and quietly suggested he take his break. Although, the bagger was slower than some of the other baggers,

there was no damage to the grocery items. In fact, many of the regular shoppers at the market oftentimes engage in friendly conversation with the bagger. What is a proactive response to this situation?

7. Restaurant. When two young good-looking men were seated in the restaurant they sat close to one another at one side of the table and held hands. The busboy provided the place settings, bread, and water. Ten minutes passed and the waiter still walked by their table without speaking to them. When one of the young men asked to order drinks, the waiter said, "I will return momentarily." Another 10 minutes passed, however, and they still had not ordered their drinks or dinners, because the waiter did not walk by their table. Their feelings of frustration were growing, yet they commented to one another that they just wanted an enjoyable dinner. Another seven minutes passed, however, and when the busboy walked by, they asked to see the manager.

Debriefing Questions

Write your answers to the debriefing questions.

1. Describe your personal reaction (feelings, thoughts) to the dialogue exercise. Did a dialogue of the case examples happen in your group? Describe.

2. What did you learn about yourself in the course of this exercise?

3. What did you learn about others in the course of this exercise?

4. Name two ways in which you can use what you have learned in daily life.

Worksheet 20

Cultural Simulation: Shodop Culture

(approx. 30 minutes)

Purpose: To practice the first three skills of cultural competence in a cultural simulation.

Instructions: Divide class into two groups, the host culture and the visiting culture. Ask the visitors to leave the room, informing them that you will meet with them momentarily to give them their instructions. Explain the rules of Shodop culture to the host group (see the Instructor's Manual). Answer any questions that arise. Next, meet with the visiting culture group and discuss their required tasks and clarify any questions. Finally, bring the groups together for interaction according to their respective roles.

Debriefing Questions

Write your answers to the debriefing questions.

1. Describe your personal reactions to Shodop culture.

2. Visitors, what do you think the rules of Shodop culture are?

3. What did you learn about yourself?

4. What did you learn about others?

5. Name two ways you can use this learning in daily life activities.

Chapter 5

Skill Four

Designing and Implementing Organizational-Cultural Competence

Designing Organizational Strategies and Action Plans

Skill Four represents a "practicing-integrating" skill that pulls together the action of the three previous skills. In this sense it becomes holistic by engaging participants in organizational problem-solving activities in which all three levels, Skills One through Three, become activated. Participants working with Skill Four techniques engage in personal, interpersonal, and systemwide thinking and skill development in the context of the practical organizational and institutional tasks they meet up with daily in their work. Skill Four is also useful in community organizing and change projects.

Skill Four is acquired by *creating case examples* and *developing action plans*. In this chapter, I first present a listing of strategies identified by organization researchers as supportive of cultural competence throughout the organization. The organization strategies are organized into two types. The first set of strategies help improve relations within the organization, among coworkers and managers/administrators and their employees. The second set of strategies are useful for improving relations external to the organization, with clients, students, customers, patients, and in community outreach and change projects. For a visual representation of cultural diversity competence and work organizations, see Figure 5.1. These organization strategies will be useful in the group activity of designing action plans, presented in Worksheets 21–23 at the end of this chapter.

FIGURE 5.1 Cultural Diversity Competence and Work Organizations

Organization Strategies

Internal Organization Strategies

The following strategies promote the development of diversity competence inside any type of organization and focus on the relations among all employees at all levels of the organization (adapted from Copeland, 1988; Fernandez, 1991; Kanter, 1977; Loden, 1996; Loden & Rosener, 1991; Morrison, 1992). Framed as a list of five general guidelines, the strategies offer possible approaches or directions an organization might take in addressing internal issues and problems in cultural diversity.

1. Maintain cultural awareness, including gender issues, at all levels of the organization.

- Provide cultural diversity training for all employees, including the CEO, supervisors, all managers, and administrators.

- Provide ongoing follow-up forums on cultural issues and problem solving.
- Provide mentoring and coaching in the identification of cultural diversity issues and in the resolution of cultural problems.
- Provide support in the formation of self-help groups and in networking among employees.
- Provide encouragement for culturally sensitive social events and the celebration of ethnic holidays.
- Establish a strategic diversity planning and implementation committee composed of representatives from all divisions, departments, and levels of the organization.
- Establish culturally diverse management and work teams.
- Incorporate a diversity training component into the orientation sessions for all new employees.
- Hire a diversity training consultant to present at least six hours of cultural diversity training to all managers each year.
- Create an office or appoint a staff manager responsible for cultural diversity issues.
- Set annual cultural diversity goals in hiring and promotion for each of the organization's divisions in both staffing and line jobs.
- Review policies to assess whether employees appreciate and support cultural diversity.
- Monitor the working procedures of employees who resist changes in discriminatory employment practices. Put simply, strict oversight is indicated, when employees have demonstrated discriminatory behavior in the past, to avoid future abuses.

2. Recruit culturally diverse employees.

- Establish ongoing outreach programs in the community to recruit culturally diverse employees. This action will establish your organization's reputation as a leader in cultural diversity competence.
- Establish a culturally diverse recruitment team whose members represent the cultural diversity of the community.
- If your organization has a college recruitment program, 10 percent of the colleges and universities it represents should have at least a 50 percent minority enrollment.
- Develop a "critical mass" or "dynamic mix" of ethnic or otherwise culturally diverse staff and clients to ensure a cultural diversity of programs in your organization.

3. Provide career development opportunities for all employees.

- Establish a mentoring, coaching, buddy system for all new employees so that learning the organization's goals, values, policies, and procedures flows more smoothly.
- Provide coaching and tutoring mechanisms to enhance individual and team effectiveness.

- Provide educational incentives and ESL (English as a second language) training as well as other language training. Fund this with tuition vouchers, if possible.
- Provide candid and accurate feedback to employees about job performance, especially in matters of cultural diversity competence.
- Establish performance evaluations based on documented achievement and results, not on personality, work style, or supervisor's personal rapport with the employee.
- Establish a system that rewards behavior that supports and makes use of cultural diversity. The formation of culturally diverse work teams would be an example of such use.
- Establish information mechanisms, such as exit interviews, for finding out why employees leave the organization.
- Encourage employees to work with new technology or to create new products, services, or processes.
- Make development planning a part of the annual goal-setting process rather than a part of performance appraisal. The latter, centered on individual whim, proves haphazard and random at best, whereas development planning as a part of organizational procedure will be more systemic and reliable.
- Establish an expenditure budget for personal self-development for every employee, which can be accessed ad hoc without a lengthy approval process.

4. **Create flexible benefit and service plans that meet the needs of culturally diverse employees.**

- Establish optional insurance plans.
- Provide information about day-care and elder-care options.
- Provide variable retirement plans—early, partial, or phased.
- Encourage employee ownership through gain-sharing, stock options, and other incentive programs.
- Provide family-friendly benefit policies, employee assistance programs, and long-term mutual commitments.
- Provide alternative work-time options such as flex-time, compressed work weeks, flex-place and telecommuting, and job sharing to accommodate employee needs.

5. **Monitor the change process.**

- Establish a system to monitor culturally diverse recruitment, career development, and promotion in the organization.
- Establish a system in the organization to monitor cultural diversity trends and issues in the local community.

External Organization Strategies

The following strategies promote the development of cultural diversity competence in an organization's external relationships (adapted from Bloom, 1997; Hogan-Garcia & Scheinberg, 2000; Hooks, 2003; Krebs

& Kunimoto, 1994; Lum, 1992, 2000; Strober, 2005). They focus on the relations of one organization with another, with culturally diverse individuals in the community at large, and with culturally diverse clients, customers, patients, or students (hereafter called clients). Framed as a list of four general guidelines, the strategies that follow offer possible approaches an organization might take in its relations with other organizations, clients, and the community at large. Generally speaking, to address cultural diversity in these relationships, the organization needs to establish wider linguistic resources for staff and the improvement of their cultural awareness, understanding, and skills. Beyond these measures, the organization will need to modify current policies and services in order to achieve a better overall "cultural fit" with culturally diverse clients, other organizations, and the community at large.

1. **Establish effective relationships with client communities.**

   - Establish a steering committee of organization staff members, culturally diverse community leaders, practitioners, and educators to facilitate program development.
   - Establish support bases with the agency administrator, governing board, and ethnic community organizations to ensure that service is provided in a culturally appropriate way.
   - Promote community organizations, such as mutual-assistance associations, to serve as vehicles for managing culturally diverse training programs in cultural awareness, understanding, and skills. Such programs in their educational thrust regularly prove effective in preventing troublesome issues and problems in cultural diversity.
   - Call on the help of indigenous community workers and natural community caretakers/leaders such as ministers, employee relatives, prominent community members, and family physicians. This practice dignifies the community and enriches the organization.
   - Study typical family structures and hierarchies to be acquainted with appropriate client kin-relationships in order to provide useful information and support resources for the organization.
   - Establish links with at least two ethnic organizations in the community for job referrals and for posting your job notices to reach their culturally diverse clients and customers.
   - Foster friendly neighborhood sharing and support services linking clients to schools, churches, and other organizations in a culturally diverse way.
   - Foster bilingual and bicultural programs as essential services in mixed ethnic or otherwise culturally diverse communities.
   - Solicit community input and participation in organization policy making. This initiative implies comprehensive orientation programs for organization board members and open access and communication between organization administration and

decision makers and community representatives. Encourage community members to provide viewpoints about their needs.

- Foster relationships that link the organization with other culturally diverse organizations for mutual information.
- Foster the development of ethnic networks within community centers to promote interaction in a bilingual and culturally diverse way that is appropriate to the community.
- Promote a highly visible presence of the organization at local restaurants, businesses, community events, and other venues of popular social interaction, to establish rapport and warm community relations.
- Locate public and private organizations that function as service agencies providing health care, day-care, and employment services near the culturally diverse communities they serve.
- Bring community and agency personnel into real dialogue using technology to provide simultaneous translation. Resulting programs will be based on the community's definition of their need and will use their strategies for intervention and prevention.

2. **Review the ethics and social responsibility of the organization.**

- Promote organization social responsibility efforts that are aimed at the overall long-term improvement of the social environment the organization provides.
- Establish criteria for measuring the organization's effect on the physical and sociocultural environment.
- Set up ethics committees for careful deliberation when complex moral issues or dilemmas arise. Such committees should typically examine available options for all parties concerned, always taking relevant issues of cultural diversity into account.
- Provide mechanisms to ensure that ethics committees in their interactions demonstrate respect for culturally diverse perspectives. They need to provide a safe environment for group members to share their varying cultural experience during the evaluation of ethical issues. Effective culturally diverse relations between the members of ethics committees themselves are essential if these groups are to engage in effective deliberation of issues that affect the community at large.
- Make it procedural for ethics committees to seek relevant information from sources external to the committee. They should take into regular account the relevant cultural perspectives of all individuals involved in the issues under examination.

3. **Strive for client satisfaction in culturally relevant ways.**

- Establish organizational programs in which personnel can truly partner with their clients.
- Initiate policies that encourage personnel to be sensitive and alert to their clients' future needs in order to better serve them.

- Establish policies that call for regular debriefing sessions for personnel in order to document information about their clients' requests.
- Establish criteria for gauging client satisfaction.

4. **Employ cultural diversity competence in serving clients** (although health care is cited, the following strategies can be tailored for use in all work sectors: human services, government, education, business, and industry).

- Encourage clients to participate actively in making decisions about their care.
- Provide culturally sensitive support groups to help clients cope with severe stress through communication. Such support groups would ideally be culturally diverse and provide relevant information about methods of service delivery, problem-solving interactions, referral services, friendly visits, and assistance in making choices about the various kinds of care available. Effective support groups help clients see themselves and their problems in a new light. In this way the support group can help its members assert a larger measure of control over their own care.
- Devise culturally diverse communication strategies for dealing with the external community in order to establish good public relations with the relevant culturally diverse population. Ideal culturally diverse strategies would provide readily intelligible information to the community in the following ways: annual reports, health education publications, press releases, or local advertisements. These strategies would also function as a conduit for information about issues in the external community pertinent to the organization, promoting coordination between the organization and key members of the external community as well.
- Make it procedural that all promotion efforts arise out of a clear understanding of and sensitivity to the diverse cultural influences on the health beliefs and practices of the target audiences (in health care organizations).
- Select target audiences with great care for cultural congruence in planning programs and campaigns to ensure maximum relevance and effect for campaign and program messages.
- Design strategies that are culturally sensitive and promote the long-term involvement of the target audience and the institutionalization of key activities within the target community when planning programs and campaigns.
- Establish a clear set of program or campaign activities and a diversity of media to promote program or campaign objectives. Price, placement, and promotion are vital factors in the selection of these activities and media. They must be *affordable* in both financial and psychological cost. They must be *attractive* to the audience, designed to grab and hold audience attention. And

they must be *informative,* explaining to the audience how, when, and where the program or campaign materials are accessible.

- Set up process evaluation procedures for monitoring and assessing program or campaign activities in order to isolate and identify efforts that require refinement. Translate the progress of the project in terms mainstream funders will understand.
- Chart a step-by-step service delivery system for culturally diverse clients. This system may call for an increase in qualified bilingual and bicultural staff, the location of more accessible facilities, or community outreach programs, for example.
- Schedule an increase of culturally appropriate services for client populations.
- Make organizational provisions for Southeast Asian, Latino, and other clients who may establish a vicarious family relationship with organization personnel. This cultural process can involve assigning a worker a position of fictive kinship within the family.
- Link with local churches, community youth centers, and schools to establish peer support groups for youths from all culture groups who have little or no family support. These links can provide functions and support analogous to the family but with a special focus on bilingual competence and education, which are important factors in all cultural settings.
- Destigmatize services by changing the names of services offered. "Mental health services," for example, could become "family outreach services."
- Provide a friendly bilingual staff, offer refreshments, and select office decor that reflects an appropriate ethnic or culturally diverse setting.
- Create organization procedures for supplying appropriate mediators from the culturally diverse community in cases in which clients are uncomfortable or unwilling to accept organization personnel as mediators.

Consider the following four health care initiatives that have proven effective among Latinos and can be adapted for all culture groups in a community:

- Spanish-language radio and television programming, a major vehicle of communication in the Chicano/Mexicano community.
- A bilingual manual of preventive health care, prepared first in Spanish and then translated into English. It retained a distinctly Chicano/Mexicano perspective.
- Educational coffee klatches and teas, called "meriendas educativas," organized from within the community to promote group mental health among low-income, Spanish-speaking women.
- Learning fairs, fiestas educativas, and all-day health workshops for high-risk Hispanics.

Table 5.1 *Anthropological Culture Change Principles*

Anthropologists' Principles for Working in Culture Change Programs

1. Planners need to begin with a comprehensive knowledge of the culture of the target community.
2. Planners need to maintain constant awareness of their own culture, particularly its relevant biases and values.
3. Baseline cultures of both the donor and recipient societies are never static, so knowledge and awareness must be current.
4. The attitudes and beliefs that had shaped previous social relations and had influenced what was borrowed or rejected in the past must be identified.
5. Proposals must meet felt needs in the recipient community.
6. Recipients must share in making decisions; planning must take account of group politics and concepts of prestige.
7. Communication among all who are involved must be facilitated.
8. Relations between acculturated and conservative members of the target community must be understood.

This list of principles is derived from numerous anthropological projects (such as the Navaho-Cornell project in which Western medicine was introduced to the Navaho Nation), *Magic, Science, and Health: The Aims and Achievements of Medical Anthropology*. Robert Anderson, Harcourt & Brace, 1996, pp. 163–172.

Table 5.1 presents eight anthropological principles for guiding community outreach and change projects.

We now turn our attention to designing an organization-wide action plan that employs all four cultural competence skills.

Writing Case Examples

Practice the technique of pulling together the specific factors that arise in real-life cultural diversity incidents. Working from personal experience covering the last year, write a case example, documenting a cultural diversity issue or problem with Worksheet 21.

Developing Action Plans

This activity provides practice devising action plans for intervening in the specific problems illustrated in the case examples—such as those written and analyzed in previous chapters. When devising action plans to remedy problems illustrated in your case examples, you will develop an organization-wide plan complete with objectives, strategies, and measures of evaluation for the three skill levels on which barriers exist. In doing so, you will engage in the process of planning that could effect real organization-wide change (see Figure 5.2). Worksheets 22 and 23 illustrate this process. Worksheet 22 provides a shorter action plan process, whereas worksheet 23 is the longer version of the activity, providing practice with personal, interpersonal, and organization-wide levels of action planning.

**Design and Implement Organization-Wide
Cultural Competence**

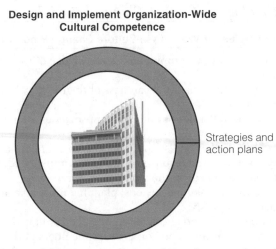

Strategies and
action plans

FIGURE 5.2 Skill Four: Design and Implement Organization-wide
Cultural Competence

Working in small groups, analyze the cultural aspects and barriers
for each case example. Your groups then need to set up a series of
actions that can be programmed into a concrete sequence of steps
for implementing a solution. The longer action plan needs to specify
timetables and evaluation measures as well. A sample of the longer
action plan is provided after Worksheet 21, "Writing a Case Example
for Use in the Action Plan" and Worksheet 22, "Short Organizational
Action Plan of Four Skills of Cultural Competence."

Worksheet 21

Writing a Case Example for Use in the Action Plan (approx. 20 minutes)

Purpose: To practice all four cultural diversity competence skills in holistic multilevel action planning for implementing cultural competence throughout the organization.

Instructions: Form groups of four or five people. Discuss a diversity issue or conflict occurring in a culturally diverse work setting within the last year. (Do this activity individually if you are taking the course online.) It can be an incident you personally experienced or something you heard about. It may have such elements of diversity as gender, ethnicity, race, age, religion, sexual orientation, physical appearance, ableness, social economic status, verbal communication, or nonverbal communication. It can be in relation to such roles as supervisor, teacher/student, salesperson/customer, health provider/patient, or coworker/coworker.

Worksheet 22

Short Organizational Action Plan of Four Skills of Cultural Competence

(approx. 30–45 minutes)

Purpose: To demonstrate the four skills of cultural diversity competence through action planning.

Instructions: Form into groups of four or five people. Discuss the answers to the following four questions in relation to your case example (Worksheet 21). For each question, let the recorder write the ideas discussed by the group. Another person needs to serve as spokesperson for your group in the whole-group discussion of each group's action plan. Do this action plan individually if you are taking this course online.

Case Example:

(Summarize the case devised in Worksheet 21)

Short Action Plan Questions

1. What levels of culture are operating in the case? What aspects of culture do you see in the case? (See Skill One in Chapter 2.)

2. What barriers do you see in the case? (See Skill Two in Chapter 3.)

3. What competencies would improve the interactions? Specify who in the case needs to practice the competencies (see Skill Three in Chapter 4).

4. What strategies would help the organization support cultural competence throughout the organization? (Use the organizational strategies discussed in the first sections of this chapter as a guide.)

5. What measures would indicate the strategies are improving the situation?

Debriefing Questions

Write your answers to the debriefing questions 2 to 6.

1. Let the spokesperson for each group present in turn their case analysis and action plan to the whole group (this question does not apply to those taking the course online).

2. Can you list any personal competencies that you found useful in carrying out this exercise?

3. Describe your personal reaction (feelings, thoughts) to the exercise. Did a dialogue in connection with the case examples occur in your group? If so, describe—this question about dialogue does not apply to those in an Internet course.

4. What did you learn about yourself in the course of this exercise?

5. What did you learn about others in the course of this exercise?

6. Name two ways in which you can use what you have learned in daily life.

Worksheet 23
Explanation of Action Plan Worksheet and Sample Action Plan

Longer Organizational Action Plan of Four Skills of Cultural Diversity Competence (approx. 60–90 minutes)

Purpose: To practice the four skills of cultural diversity competence in action plan development for implementing cultural competence throughout the organization.

Case Example:

Summarize on this worksheet the main points of the case example previously developed in Worksheet 21.

Analysis of Cultural Aspects and Barriers

Describe the aspects and levels of culture and barriers relevant to the diversity issues in the case example.

1. Personal and Interpersonal Level

Objectives and Goals

Identify an objective or goal that would improve the interaction in the case example.

Identify the competencies that would improve the interaction in the case example (Skill Three).

Action Steps

Identify specific activities that promote the achievement of the objective (use the organization strategies described previously).

Timetable

Set up a schedule for achieving the objective.

Measures of Progress

Identify specific measures that demonstrate achievement of the objective.

2. Organizational Level

Objectives and Goals

Discuss and identify an organizational objective or goal.

Action Steps

Specify activities that promote the achievement of the objective (use the organization strategies discussed previously).

Timetable

Set up a schedule for carrying out the action.

Measures of Progress

Identify specific measures that demonstrate the achievement of the objective.

Sample Case Example and Action Plan

Case Example:

A school with a large Hispanic population is planning to celebrate Cinco de Mayo with strolling mariachi musicians. The classroom teachers spend time preparing the children for the classroom visits of the mariachis. However, during the event, the musicians skip some of the classrooms with fewer Hispanic children. The children in these classrooms feel left out and disappointed.

Cultural Aspects and Barriers

In this case example we can identify two aspects of culture: art and expressive forms and social group interaction patterns. Stereotyping, verbal barriers, judgment, stress, and organizational barriers are also to be noted. The children in the classrooms not visited by the mariachis feel disappointed, neglected, and devalued by the school. The school fails to include all the children in all the classes, which gives rise to the central problem, lack of inclusion.

1. Personal and Interpersonal Level

Objectives and Goals

The following personal competencies are relevant in this case example: All employees at the school need to show empathy. To listen carefully. To manage personal biases and stereotypes. To be nonjudgmental. To assume complexity. To be flexible. To show respect. To be resourceful.

Action Steps

Provide cultural competence training for everyone in the school.

Timetable

Call an in-service before the semester begins in fall.

Measures of Progress

Surveys indicate all students feel included in school activities and feel valued by the school staff. The staff feels positive about working at the school. They feel part of an important team. These measures of progress should be documented.

2. Organizational Level

Objectives and Goals

Design school programs that are wholly inclusive.

Action Steps

- Recruit diverse employees.
- Create a central school area featuring a calendar and perhaps a globe that show how all groups are represented and how all groups figure in the larger picture.
- Hold school cultural awareness assemblies for everyone's active participation.
- Encourage students to write essays about cultural awareness problems, incidents, and issues.
- Sponsor culturally sensitive films with follow-up discussions that pinpoint relevant diversity issues.
- Promote cultural awareness projects, especially those that demonstrate how it feels to be "somebody else."

Timetable

Schedule cultural events for three-month intervals throughout the school year.

Measures of Progress

- Surveys showing parent involvement
- Student responses on essays documenting how included they may or may not feel
- Teacher evaluations documenting their views of the program and its success
- Documentation of the decrease of student behavioral problems as an indicator of progress

Case Example and Action Plan Worksheet (longer version, approx. 60–90 minutes)

Case Example Summary (summarize case example devised in Worksheet 21)

Cultural Aspects and Barriers analysis

Action Plan

1. Personal and Interpersonal Level

    Objectives and Goals

    Action Steps

    Timetable

    Measures of Progress

2. Organizational Level

    Objectives and Goals

    Action Steps

    Timetable

    Measures of Progress

Debriefing Questions

Write your answers to the debriefing questions 2 through 6.

1. Let the spokesperson for each group present in turn their case analysis and action plan to the whole group.

2. Can you list any personal competencies that you found in your command in carrying out this exercise?

3. Describe your personal reaction (feelings, thoughts) to the exercise. Did a dialogue in connection with the case examples occur in your group? If so, describe.

4. What did you learn about yourself in the course of this exercise?

5. What did you learn about others in the course of this exercise?

6. Name two ways in which you can use what you have learned in daily life

Conclusion

The four skills covered in this book provide a proactive and holistic approach to implementing cultural competence at the personal, inter-personal, and organization levels. The four skills process utilizes both conceptual and practical tools. The first skill, understanding culture as multilevel, fosters a nonstatic, dynamic understanding of culture. Working with the 12 aspects of culture deepens awareness and under-standing of the multidimensional nature of culture. The second skill, understanding the six barriers to effective relationships, provides a conceptual tool for recognizing cultural dynamics that surface in group patterns of social interaction. Skills One and Two combined foster cultural awareness and understanding, called culture-mindedness. In Skill Three, the focus is on culturally centered communication at the personal and interpersonal levels with practice of the 14 personal competencies, the dialogue, conflict recovery, and problem-solving processes. Skill Four builds on the first three skills in organization problem solving useful in strategic planning for implementing organization-wide cultural competence. This book will be useful to everyone throughout his or her life because cultural competence is a necessity for living in our culturally diverse societies. It is my intent for those who have engaged in the four-skills process presented in this book to recognize that cultural competence is a relation process of social flexibility for living and thriving in our culturally diverse societies.

Appendix

Aspects of U.S. Mainstream/ National Culture

1. History: Mainstream culture in the United States derives from Anglo-core culture of the English who colonized America.

2. Social Group Interaction Patterns
    - Intragroup: English immigrants institutionalized English culture in the United States.
    - Intergroup: Starting in colonial times, white members of U.S. national culture display "nativism" toward groups perceived as different (antiforeign, anti-Semitic, anti-Catholic, antiblack).

3. Social Status: Middle-class culture is the norm, yet there are a range of classes—poverty, working, middle, and upper class. Since the 1970s the upper and poor classes have been growing, with the middle class declining.

4. Value Orientations: Emphasis on
    - patriarchal nuclear family
    - doing, "getting things done" (keeping busy)
    - measurable and visible accomplishments
    - individual choice, responsibility, and achievement
    - self-reliance and self-motivation
    - pragmatism: "if an idea works, use it"
    - "the new" (and change)
    - causal agent; things do not just happen
    - equality, informality, and fair play simultaneously with widespread nativism and micro and macro institutional discrimination
    - competition

- direct communication
- controlling nature; nature "should" serve humans
- materialism, machines and technology, and progress
- private property (is valued more than human rights)

5. Language and Communication
    - verbal: English language spoken; most do not speak second language, nor is it valued
    - low context communication style: direct, explicit, and informal
    - nonverbal: not recognized as important as verbal communication
    - emphasis on precise reckoning of time, which is perceived as lineal

6. Family Life Processes: Traditionally, patriarchal nuclear family structure. Currently much variation in family structure due to economic change affecting families. Two-paycheck families are the norm.
    - gender roles: traditionally male job holder, female homemaker, but changing gender roles since 1960s
    - occupations: varies with socioeconomic status (with fewer industrial jobs and more service and information jobs since 1970s economic restructuring and the growth of globalization)
    - education: varies with socioeconomic status
    - marriage customs: changing; marriage in later 20s increasing
    - divorce practice: high rate of divorce and serial monogamy common
    - parenting beliefs and practices: emphasize individualism, self-reliance, and competition

7. Healing Beliefs and Practices: biomedical model promoted

8. Religion: Protestant religions, biblical tradition emphasized

9. Art and Expressive Forms: music and visual art emphasized, not verbal arts, for example

10. Diet: hamburgers, hot dogs, but diets vary by regions and ethnicity

11. Recreation: sports, TV, and many other options (much variation)

12. Clothes: styles change in time and place (region)

By Mikel Hogan.
Adapted from: L. D. Baker, ed., *Life in America: Identity and Everyday Experience.* Blackwell Publishing (2004).
Susan Hegeman, *Patterns for America.* Princeton University Press (1999).
Dan Rose, *Patterns of American Culture.* University of Pennsylvania Press (1989).
Edward Stewart and Milton Bennet, *American Cultural Patterns.* Intercultural Press (1991).
Robert Bellah et al., *Habits of the Heart.* Harper & Row (1985).
John Hodge et al., *The Cultural Basis of Racism.* Two Rider's Press, Berkeley, CA. (1975).

Sample Syllabus and Reading Resources for Term Paper

Human Services 311

Intracultural Socialization

Off. Hrs: Wed. 1–5; Thur. 1–4

Phone: (714) 278-330

Mikel Hogan, Ph.D.

Ec-478

email: mhogan@fullerton.edu

Introduction and Course Description

In the last 20 years the shift from an industrial to an information and service economy has been complete. The nature of the new economy is one of increased complexity and change, prompting one researcher, in fact, to label our current era the "era of dynamic complexity" (Ralph Kilman, *Beyond the Quick Fix*). In addition to vast economic and social structural change, our society has changed in composition over the last 20 years. In addition to the traditional culturally diverse groups that compose U.S. society, there is an influx of new immigrants from Latin America and Asia combined with the "graying" of America. Thus, our communities (schools, workforce, for example) are becoming even more socioculturally diverse. Cultural awareness, understanding, and new interpersonal skills are a vital competency required for effective functioning in our dynamic and diverse society. This course is designed to provide a first step toward developing that competence.

Learning Objectives

To increase students' awareness and understanding of:

- United States national culture, organization culture, racial/ethnic and other subcultures.
- Personal culture (core identity).
- Theories of diversity.
- The history of racial, ethnic, class, gender, ableness, and other diversity experiences.
- Diverse social relations and how they are affected by the present political, economic, and social context of the United States.
- The life experience of an individual member of a specific group as expressed in his/her own words.

Teaching Methods

The learning tasks (text readings, exams, written papers) required for the grade in this class are designed to promote both cognitive and affective learning. Students will gain much new knowledge and a personal grounding of the intellectual mastery of the subject matter. They will also explore their own beliefs, values, feelings, and life experience in relation to the race, ethnic, gender, socioeconomic concepts, and issues to which they are exposed during the semester. Learning, I believe, is most potent and meaningful when it affects a student directly.

The in-class activities, moreover, will promote the development of critical thinking in students. Critical thinking is important for solving problems, working toward our goals, understanding information and understanding people. In-class activities will emphasize small and large group discussions and problem solving in relation to case examples and case studies drawn from the work sector and communities at large.

Texts

Understanding Human Differences. By Kent Koppelman with R. Lee Goodhart. Pearson, 2005.

The Four Skills of Cultural Diversity Competence. By Mikel Hogan. Wadsworth/Brooks/Cole, 2006.

Grading Policy

There are 485 points for the class (see explanation below). Course grade is based on the following: Approximately 90%–99% of 485 will earn an "A," 80%–89% a "B," 70%–79% a "C," and so on.

1. **Readings and Classroom Participation.** Students are expected to read the texts and integrate materials from the text and lectures. Although the class is large in number, discussion is expected and encouraged. Good attendance can be the determining factor when grade points are borderline.

2. **Exams.** There will be two midterms and a final exam (short answer and objective). Study sheets will be provided. The exams are based on the study sheet information (**300 points**).

3. **Required Homework and Term Paper:**

   A. Each student is required to write the answers to worksheets contained in the Hogan text. These worksheets provide an opportunity to personally deepen your understanding of the dynamic complexity of cultural processes. Write your worksheet in pen, copy (Xerox) the completed worksheet from the book, and submit the copy to me (see the Weekly Schedule for the worksheet due dates). Each worksheet is worth 5 points for a total of **85 points.**

   B. Each student is required to write a 12-page (typed, double-spaced) analysis of a narrative written by a member of a diverse group. The format of the analysis is the "aspects of culture/

ethnicity" presented in Chapter 2 of the Hogan text. A useful bibliography of potential narratives is provided in the Resources Section. The paper is worth **100 points.**

Aspects of Culture/Ethnicity Paper: Instructions

Part I Introduction

A. Brief description of overview of book's main storyline and characters.

B. Statement describing what will be presented in the paper.

Part II Sociocultural Analysis (Using Aspects of Culture)

Choose three of the Aspects of Culture/Ethnicity (presented in Chapter 2 of Hogan text) and tell in your narrative the reason they were selected. Use quotes from the book to illustrate the reason you chose the three aspects. Document each quote by putting the page number from the book in parentheses. This cultural analysis aims at teaching you a method for obtaining cultural data on an "emic" or insider viewpoint. By reading a book written by a person outside your social group, you are "walking in another's shoes," so to speak. This experience helps you learn cultural competence for working and living in a culturally diverse society/world.

Part III Conclusion

Briefly summarize what you've presented and tell your personal reaction. What did you learn, were your attitudes influenced by what you learned, is there a practical way in which you can apply what you learned in the nursing profession?

Grading Criteria for Aspects of Culture/Ethnicity Paper

Paper should contain the following sections: (100 points total)

1. Introduction Section—20 points

2. Aspects of Culture/Ethnicity (3 aspects discussed)—40 points

3. Documentation (all quotes need page number in parentheses)—15 points

4. Conclusion Section—15 points

5. Written in a well-organized and logical manner—10 points

Turn in *2 copies* of your paper if you want one returned to you.

Note: There are a variety of extra-credit options.

Weekly Schedule

Week	Topic	Assignment
1	Introduction: context and need for cultural diversity competence	Read Hogan, ch. 1 & 2; Write worksheets 1, 2, 3, & 5; Read Koppelman, Preface & ch. 1
2 & 3	Practicing skills 1 & 2: understanding culture as multilevel and the barriers to effective relationships Films: "ASCO": L.A. Performance Artists	Read Hogan, ch. 3 & 4; Write worksheets 6–10; Read Koppleman, ch. 2
4 & 5	Practicing skill 3: culturally centered communication Films: "Ellis Island"; "Slavery's Buried Past"	Write Hogan worksheets 12, 13, 14, 17, 18, & 19; Read Kopplelman, ch. 3 & 4
6 & 7	Practicing skill 4: Action planning for organization/community change **Midterm exam 1** (6th week, covers Hogan 1–5; Koppelman, 1–4)	Read Hogan, ch. 5; Write worksheets 21 & 23; Read Koppelman, ch. 5 & 6
8 & 9	Cultural Foundations of Oppression in the United States Film: "Ancestors in America"	Read Koppleman, ch. 7–9
10 & 11	Barriers in Social Group Interaction Patterns: racism, sexism, & heterosexism Film: "Storytellers of the Pacific"	Read Koppleman, 10–11
12 & 13	Barriers in Social Group Interaction Patterns: classism & ableism **Midterm exam 2** (12th week, covers Koppleman, 5–10)	Read Koppleman, ch. 12–13
14 & 15	Organizational/Institutional and Community Cultural Competence Films: "Days of Waiting"; "American Sons"	Read Koppleman, ch. 14 & 15
16	Review for final exam	
17	Final exam	

Resources for Term Paper

Selected Bibliography of Insiders' Accounts on Race, Ethnicity, Gender, Ableness, and Class Experience in the United States

General Collections

This Bridge We Call Home. Gloria Anzuldua and AnaLouise Keating. Harper, 2002.

Inside Separate Worlds. David Schoem, ed. University of Michigan Press, 1991. Life stories of young blacks, Jews, and Latinos.

Making Face, Making Soul: Creative and Critical Perspectives by Women of Color. Gloria Anzalua, ed. Aunt Lute Foundation Books, 1990.

To Serve the Devil. Paul Jacobs, Saul Landau with Eve Pell, eds. Vintage Books, 1971. Collection of documentary analysis on America's racial and ethnic history. Two volumes. Vol. I: American Indians, Blacks, and Chicanos. Vol. II: Hawaiian, Chinese, Japanese, and Puerto Ricans.

Unequal Sisters. Ellen Carol DuBois and Vicki L. Ruiz, eds. Routledge Press, 1990. A multicultural reader in U.S. women's history.

Ableness

A Place for Noah. Josh Greenfeld. Harcourt, Brace, Jovanovich, 1978.

Beyond Ramps. Marta Russell, Common Courage Press, 1998.

Disability and Culture. B. Ingstad and S. Whyte, eds. University of California Press, 1995.

Disability in Different Cultures. B. Holzer, A. Vreede, and G. Weigt. Transaction, 1999.

Down is Up for Aron: A Mother's Spiritual Journey with Down Syndrome. M. Noble. Harper, 1993.

Evidence of Harm. D. Kirby. St. Martin's Press, 2005.

The New Disability History. P. Longmore and L. Umansky, eds. New York University Press, 2001.

Nothing about Us without Us. J. Charlton. University of California Press, 2000.

Perspectives in Disability. M. Nagler. Health Markets Research, 1993.

Rethinking Disability. P. Devlieger, F. Rusch, and D. Pfeiffer. Garant, 2003.

Thinking in Pictures and Other Reports from My Life with Autism. T. Grandlin. Doubleday, 1995.

Toward a Poetics of the Disabled Body. R. Garland-Thomson. Pearson, 2000.

Train Go Sorry: Inside a Deaf World. L. H. Cohen. Houghton Mifflin, 1994.

African Americans

Alice Walker's novels (all apply).

Bearing the Cross: Martin Luther King Jr. and the Southern Christian Leadership Conference. David J. Garrow. First Vintage Books Edition, 1988.

Beloved. Toni Morrison. Alfred A. Knopf, 1987.

The Big Sea. Langston Hughes. An autobiographic book by a Harlem Renaissance writer.

Brown Girl, Brown Stones, a Novel. Paule Marshall. Feminist Press, 1981.

The Chosen Place, the Timeless People. Paule Marshall. Vintage Contemporaries, 1969. Novel that provides insight into the political-economic structure and history of black and white relations in Jamaica (with some reference to the U.S. black experience), and, through the voice of Merle, the novel provides a "native's" view of anthropological fieldwork.

The Color Purple. Alice Walker. Washington Square Press, 1982. A historical novel about African and Afro-American experience as perceived and told by a southern black woman.

Dry-Long-So. A Self-Portrait of Black America. John Gwaltney. Vintage Books, 1981.

The Habit of Surviving. Kesho Yvonne Scott. Ballantine Books, 1991. Five extraordinary women share the conflicts and struggles that define their lives as black women in America.

The Big Sea by Langston Hughes, New York, Alfred Knopf, Inc. 1940.

The Invisible Man. Ralph Ellison. Bantam Books, 1957.

James Baldwin novels (all apply).

Killers of the Dream. Lillian Smith. Norton, 1949. Reprint 1961. About life in the segregated South.

Lay Bare the Heart: An Autobiography of the Civil Rights Movement. James Farmer. New American Library, 1986.

Lemon Swamp and Other Places. A Carolina Memoir. Mamie Garvin Fields with Karen Fields. Free Press, 1983.

Like One of the Family. Alice Childress. Beacon Press, 1986 (first published in 1956). Through the conversations between Mildred, a black domestic, and her friend Marge, the author presents a vibrant picture of the "life of a Black woman working in New York in the 1950s."

Mama Day. Gloria Naylor. Ticknor and Fields, 1988.

Meridian. Alice Walker. Washington Square Press, 1976. A historical novel about the voters' rights drive in the 1950s South, written from the perspective of a southern black woman.

The Montgomery Bus Boycott and the Women Who Started It: The Memoir of Jo Ann Gibson Robinson. David J. Garrow, ed. University of Tennessee Press, 1987.

My Soul Is Rested: The Story of the Civil Rights Movement in the Deep South. Howell Raines. Viking Penguin Books, 1983. Collections of interviews with people who were (are) involved in the civil rights movement.

A Nation of Lords: The Autobiography of the Vice Lords. David Dawley. Doubleday Anchor, 1973. An account of the evolution of a gang on Chicago's West Side. "The Vice Lords speak for themselves about where they have been and where they are going."

Plum Bun: A Novel without a Moral. Jessie Redmon Fauset. Pandora Press, 1985. Jessie Fauset, a Harlem Renaissance writer, first wrote this novel about "passing" in the 1920s.

Paule Marshall novels (all apply).

Praise Song for the Widow. Paule Mashall. E. P. Dutton Press, 1984.

Re'lize Whut Ahm Talkin' Bout? Steve Chennault. Angel Press, 1980.

Selma, Lord, Selma: Girlhood Memories of the Civil Rights Days. Sheyann Webb and Rachel West Nelson as told to Frank Sikora. William Morrow, 1980.

In Search of Naunny's Grave. Nick Truhillo, AltaMira Press, 2004.

The Temple of My Familiar. Alice Walker. Harcourt, Brace, Jovanovich, 1989.

Toni Morrison novels (all apply).

We Are Your Sisters. Dorothy Sterling, ed. Norton, 1984. Documents on black women in the 19th century. The documents derive from the experience of women in slavery times (both slave and free), the Civil War, and postwar years.

When I Was Coming Up: An Oral History of Aged Blacks. Audrey Olsen Faulkner, Marsel A. Heisel, Wendell Holbrook, and Shirley Geismar. Shoestring Press, 1982.

You May Plow Here: The Narrative of Sara Brooks. Thordis Simonsen, ed. A Touchstone Book, 1983.

Zora Neal Hurston novels (all apply).

American Indian/Indigenous Peoples

American Indian Women Telling Their Lives. Gretchen M. Bataille and Kathleen Mullen Sands. University of Nebraska Press, 1984.

Black Elk Speaks. Being the Life Story of a Holyman among the Oglala Sioux. John Neihardt. Pocket Books, 1972.

Bury My Heart at Wounded Knee: An Indian History of the American West. Dee Brown. Bantam Books, 1970.

Children of the Sun: Stories by and about Indian Kids. Adolf and Beverly Hungry Wolf. William Morrow, 1987.

Custer Died for Your Sins: An Indian Manifesto. Vine Deloria, Jr. Avon, 1969.

Custer's Fall, the Indian Side of the Story. David Humphreys Miller. Bison Printing, 1985.

God is Red. Vine Deloria, Jr. Delta Books, 1973.

Daughters of Copperwoman. Anne Cameron. Press Gang, 1981.

Daughters of the Earth: The Lives and Legends of the American Indian Women. Carolyn Niethammer. Macmillan, 1977.

From Indians to Chicanos, 2nd ed. James Diego Vigil. Waveland Press, 1998.

In Search of the Old Ones. David Roberts, Touchstone, 1997.

Oglala Women. Myth, Ritual, and Reality. Marla N. Powers. University of Chicago Press, 1986.

The Powwow Highway. David Seals. A Plume Book, 1979.

Red Sand, Blue Sky. Kathy Applegate. Feminist Press, 2000.

Sanapia. Comanche Medicine Woman. David E. Jones. Waveland Press, 1984.

Tony Hillerman novels about Hopi and Navaho (all apply).

A Voice in Her Own Tribe: A Navajo Woman's Own Story. Irene Stewart. Ballena Press, 1974.

The Ways of My Grandmothers. Beverly Hungry Wolf. Quill, 1980.

We Are Mesquakie, We Are One. Hadley Irwin. Feminist Press, 2003.

The Woman at Otowi Crossing. Frank Waters. Sage/Swallow Press Books, 1970.

The Zuni Enigma. Nancy Yaw Davis. Norton, 2001.

Asian Americans
Two collections of readings by Asian Americans about their experiences, published by the UCLA Asian American Studies Center:

Roots: An Asian American Reader. UCLA, 1971.

Counterpoint: Perspectives on Asian Americans. UCLA, 1976.

Asian American Youth: Culture, Identity, and Ethnicity. Jennifer Lee and Min Zhou. Routledge, 2004.

Asian Woman. Asian Women's Journal, UC Berkeley, 1971.

Chinese American Portraits. Personal Histories 1828–1988. Ruthamme Lum McCunn. Chronicle Books, 1988.

The Floating World. Cynthia Kadohata. Ballantine Books, 1989.

Hearts of Sorrow: Vietnamese American Lives. James Freeman. Stanford University Press, 1989.

The Hundred Secret Senses. Amy Tan. Ivy Books, 1995.

The Joy Luck Club. Amy Tan. Ivy Books, 1989.

The Kitchen God's Wife. Amy Tan. Ivy Books, 1991.

Long Time California: A Documentary Study of an American Chinatown. Victor G. and Brett DeBary Nee. Houghton Mifflin, 1974.

No No Boy. John Okada. American Resources Project, San Francisco, CA. 1976. Nisei viewpoint of post–WW II Japanese experiences in Northwest United States.

Rice Bowl Women: Writings by and about the Women of China and Japan. Dorothy Blair Shimer, ed. New American Library, 1982.

The Sacred Willow. Duong Van Mai Elliott. Oxford University Press, 1999.

Through Harsh Winters: The Life of a Japanese Immigrant Woman. Akemi Kikumura. Chandler and Sharp, 1981.

To Live and to Write: Selections by Japanese Women Writers 1913–1938. Yukiko Tanaka, ed. Seal Press, 1987.

Warrior Lessons. P. Eng. Pocket books, 1999.

With Silk Wings: Asian Americans at Work. Elaine H. Kim with Janice Otani. Asian Women United of California, 1983.

The Woman Warrior. Maxine Hong Kingston. Alfred Knopf, 1977.

Asian Indians

Karma Cola: Marketing the Mystic East. Gita Mehta. Fawcett Columbine, 1979.

Motiba's Tattos. Mira Kamador. Plume Printing, 2001.

The Namesake. Jhumpa Lahira. Houghton, 2003.

Filipinos

America Is in the Heart. Carlos Bulosan. Bantam Books, 1976.

Gay/Lesbian/Bisexual/Transgender

On Being Gay. Brian McNaught. St. Martin Press, 1988.

Beyond Acceptance. Carolyn Welch Griffin et al., Prentice Hall, 1986.

Coming Out, An Act of Love. Rob Eichberg. Plum, 1991.

Coming Out to Parents. Mary Borheck. Pilgrim Press, Revised 1990.

The Family of Woman. Maureen Sullivan. University of California Press, 2004.

A Home at the End of the World. Michael Cunningham. Picador, 1990.

A Member of the Family: Gay Men Write about Their Families. John Preston, ed. Plum, 1992.

The Original Coming Out Stories. Penelope Wolfe, ed. Plum, 1989.

Queer Ideas. David Kessler. Feminist Press, 2003.

Hispanics, Latinos, and Chicano Americans

Cannery Women. Cannery Lives: Mexican Women, Unionization, and the California Food Processing Industry, 1930–1950. Vicki L. Ruiz. University of New Mexico Press, 1987.

Children of NAFTA. David Bacon. University of California Press, 2004.

Crossing Over: A Mexican Family on the Migrant Trail. Ruben Martinez. Picador, 2001.

Cuban Americans: Masters of Survival. Jose Llanes. Abt Books, 1982. The Cuban American experience based on interviews with 187 Cuban Americans.

Family Installments: Memories of Growing Up Hispanic. Edward Rivera. Penguin Books, 1982.

Famous All Over Town. Danny Santiago. An adolescent's experience in L.A.'s barrio. Delta, 1982.

The Glass Window. Mario Morales. Authors Choice Press, 2003. Growing up in Southern California of the 1950s.

Growing Up Puerto Rican. Paulette Cooper, ed. Arbor House, 1972. Collection of narratives of Puerto Ricans telling about their childhood and adolescent experiences.

Las Mujeres: Conversations from a Hispanic Community. An Oral History. Nan Elsasser and Yvonne Tixier y Vigil. Feminist Press, 1980.

Macho. Victor Villasenor. Delta, 1991.

The Moths and Other Stories. Helena Maria Viramontes. Arte Publico Press, 1985. Collection of stories derived from growing body of literature written by Chicanas and Latinas in this country.

New Mexico Women: Intercultural Perspectives. Joan M. Jensen and Darlis A. Miller, eds. University of New Mexico Press, 1986.

The Revolt of the Cockroach People. Oscar Zeta Acosta. Bantam Books, 1974.

Sueno de Colibri: Hummingbird Dream. A Collection of Poems. Naomi Quinonez. West End Press, 1985.

Trini. E. Portillo Trambley. Feminist Press, 2005.

Woman on the Edge of Time. Marge Piercy. Fawcett Crest Books. Novel based on interviews of inmates in mental institution. Chicana is the heroine in the context of the 1950s.

Yucatecans in Dallas Texas. Rachel Adler. Pearson, 2004.

Jewish Americans

An Estate of Memory. Ilona Karmel. Feminist Press, 2002.

Bread Givers. Anzia Yezierska. Doubleday Press, 1925.

The Downtown Jews: Portraits of an Immigrant Generation. Ronald Sanders. Dover, 1979.

The House of Memory. Marjorie Agosin. Helen Rose Scheur Series, 2004.

Keepers of the History. E. Young. Teachers College Press, 1992.

Number Our Days. Barbara Meyerhoff. Touchstone, 1978.

The Shalom Seders. Three Haggadahs. Complied by New Jewish Agenda, 1984.

Middle Eastern Americans

The Arab-American Community in Detroit, Michigan. S. Gold. Pearson, 2002.

Baghdad Burning: Girl Blog from Iraq. Anonymous. Feminist Press, 2003.

Before the Flames: A Quest for the History of Arab Americans. Greg Orfalea. University of Texas Press. 1988.

Hollywood's Muslim Arabs. J. Shaheen. Pearson, 2000.

The Kite Runner, K. Hosseini. Penguin, 2003.

Night Draws Near. Anthony Shadid. Penguin, 2005.

On Shifting Ground: Middle Eastern Women in the Global Era. F. Nourie-Simone. Feminist Press, 2005.

Touba and the Meaning of Night. S. Parsipur. Feminist Press, 2006.

Men

The American Male. Elizabeth H. Pleck and Joseph H. Pleck. Prentice Hall, 1980.

The Flying Boy. John Lee. Health Communications, 1989.

King, Warrior, Magician, Lover: Rediscovering the Archetypes of the Mature Masculine. Robert Moore and Douglas Gillette. Harper, 1991.

The Male Machine. Marc Feign Fasteau. McGraw-Hill, 1973.

Men and Masculinity. Joseph H. Peck and Jack Sawyer, eds. Prentice Hall, 1974.

Men's Studies Modified: The Impact of Feminism on the Academic Disciplines. Dale Spender, ed. Pergamon Press, 1981.

The Mind at Work. Mike Rose. Viking Penguin, 2004.

The Myth of Masculinity. Joseph H. Pleck. MIT Press, 1981.

White Like Me: Reflections on Race from a Privileged Son. Tim Wise. Soft Skull Press, 2005.

The Will to Change: Men, Masculinity, and Love. B. Hooks. Washington Square Press, 2004.

Mixed Race/Ethnic Identity

Cross-Addressing. John Hawley. State University of New York, 1996.

Does Anybody Else Look Like Me? Donna Jackson Nakazawa. Perseus, 2003.

The Future Is Mestizo. Virgilio Elizondo. University of Colorado Press, 2000.

Mavin: The Mixed Race Experience. Journal features "insider" resources 1995–2005; www.mavinfoundation.org.

New Faces in a Changing America: Multiracial Identity in the 21st Century. Loretta Winters and Herman DeBose. Sage, 2003.

No Passing Zone: The Artistic and Discursive Voices of Asian-Descent Multiracials. Velina Hasu Houston and Teresa Williams. *Amerasia Journal,* Vol. 23, No. 1, 1997.

The Sum of Our Parts: Mixed Heritage Asian Americans. Teresa Williams-Leon and Cynthia Nakashima, eds. Temple University Press, 2001.

Women

All about Love: New Visions. B. Hooks. Perennial, 2000.

Communion: The Female Search for Love. B. Hooks. HarperCollins, 2002.

Composing a Life. Mary Catherine Bateson. Plume, 1990.

Erin's Daughter in America: Irish Immigrant Women in the Nineteenth Century. Hasia R. Diner. John Hopkins University Press, 1983.

Fathers. Reflections by Daughters. Ursula Owen, ed. Pantheon Books, 1983.

Global Woman: Nannies, Maids, and Sex Workers in the New Economy. B. Ehrenreich and A. R. Hoschschild, eds. Henry Holt, 2002.

Hillbilly Women. Kathy Kahn. Avon Books, 1973.

If All We Did Was to Weep at Home: A History of White Working Class Women in America. Susan Estabrook Kennedy. Indiana University Press, 1979.

I'm on My Way Running: Women Speak on Coming of Age. Lyn Reese, Jean Wilkinson, and Phyliss Sheon Kippelman, eds. Avon Books, 1983.

The Mind at Work. Mike Rose. Viking Penguin, 2004.

Mothers of the South: Portraiture of the White Tenant Farm Woman. Margaraet Jarman Hagood. Norton, 1977.

Moving the Mountain: Women Working for Social Change. Ellen Cantarow. Feminist Press, 1980.

Outside the Magic Circle: The Autobiography of Virginia Foster Durr. Hollinger F. Barnard, ed. University of Alabama Press, 1985.

The Parish and the Hill. Mary Doyle Curran. Feminist Press, 2003.

The Red-Haired Girl from the Bog. Patricia Monaghan. New World Library, 2003.

Revolution from Within. Gloria Steinem. Little Brown, 1992.

Rosie the Riveter Revisited: Women, the War and Social Change. Sherna Berger Gluck. New American Library, 1987.

That's How It Was. Maureen Duffy. Dial Press, 1984.

Westward the Women: An Anthology of Western Stories by Women. Vicki Piekarski, ed. University of New Mexico Press, 1984.

Windbreak: A Woman Rancher on the Northern Plains. Linda Hasselstrom. Barn Owl Books, 1987.

With These Hands: Women Working on the Land. Joan M. Jensen. Feminist Press, 1981.

A Woman's Place: The Life History of a Rural Ohio Grandmother. Rosemary O. Joyce. Ohio State University Press, 1983.

Women in Kentucky. Helen Deiss Irvin. University Press of Kentucky, 1979.

Working Wives/Working Husbands. Joseph H. Pleck. Sage, 1985.

References

Alba, R. (1990). *Ethnic identity. The transformation of white America.* New Haven, CT: Yale University Press.

Anderson, R. (1996). *Magic, science, and health: The aims and achievements of medical anthropology.* New York: Harcourt & Brace.

Anzaldua, G. (1990). *Making face, making soul.* San Francisco: Aunt Lute Foundation Books.

Arensberg, C. A. (1987). Theoretical contributions of industrial and development studies. In E. M. Eddy & W. L. Partridge (Eds.), *Applied anthropology in America.* New York: Columbia University Press.

Arvizu, S. (2001). Building bridges and empowerment: Anthropological contributions to diversity and educational practices. In I. Susser & T. C. Patterson (Eds.), *Cultural diversity in the United States.* Malden, MA: Blackwell.

Aveni, A. (2002). *Empires of time: Calendars, clocks, and cultures.* Boulder: University Press of Colorado.

Bach, R. (1993). *Changing relations: Newcomers and established residents in the United States community.* New York: Ford Foundation.

Baker, L. D. (Ed.). (2004). *Life in America: Identity and everyday experience.* Berlin, Germany: Blackwell.

Baker, Lee D., & Patterson, Thomas C. (Eds.). (1994). Special issue: Race, racism, and the history of U.S. anthropology. *Transforming Anthropology, 5,* 1–41.

Banks, J. A. (1988). *Multiethnic education: Theory and practice.* Newton, MA: Allyn & Bacon.

Banks, J. A. (1989). *Multicultural education: Issues and perspectives.* Newton, MA: Allyn & Bacon.

Barak, M. (2000). The inclusive workplace: An ecosystems approach to diversity management. *Social Work, 45*(4), 339–355.

Barth, F. (1968, 1998). *Ethnic groups and boundaries.* Prospect Heights, IL: Waveland Press.

Bashkow, I. (2004). A neo-Boasian conception of cultural boundaries. *American Anthropologist, 106*(3), 443–458.

Batteau, A. (2000). Negations and ambiguities in the cultures of organizations. *American Anthropologist, 102*(4), 726–741.

Behrens, Debra Peters. (1996). Beyond awareness: An action science approach to cross-cultural relations, a prolegomenon. *Advances in Confluent Education, 1,* 95–112.

Bell, R. (1979). *Sturdy black bridges.* Garden City, NY: Anchor Books.

Black, J. S., & Mendenhall, M. (1989). A practical but theory-based framework for selecting cross-cultural training methods. *Human Resource Management, 28,* 511–539.

Bloom, S. (1997). *Creating sanctuary: Toward an evolution of sane societies.* New York: Routledge.

Bodley, John H. (2001). *Anthropology and contemporary human problems* (4th ed.). Mountain View, CA: Mayfield.

Bowie, F. (2000). *The anthropology of religion.* Oxford, England: Blackwell.

Brameld, T. (1965). Anthropotherapy—toward theory and practice. *Human Organization, 24*(4), 288–297.

Brink, P. (1990). *Transcultural nursing.* Prospect Heights, IL: Waveland Press.

Brislen, R. (1986). *Intercultural interactions: A practical guide.* Beverly Hills, CA: Sage.

Brookfield, S. (1990). *The skillful teacher.* San Francisco: Jossey-Bass.

Buck, Pem Davidson, & D'Amico-Samuels, Deborah. (Eds.). (1991). Special issue: Teaching as praxis: Race and ideologies of power. *Transforming Anthropology, 2*(1), 1–43.

Burden, D., & Gottlieb, N. (Eds.). (1987). *The woman client.* New York: Tavistock Publications.

Calasanti, T. M., & Slevin, K. F. (2001). *Gender, social inequalities and aging.* Walnut Creek, CA: AltaMira Press.

Carrico, R. L. (1987). *Strangers in a stolen land.* Newcastle, CA: Sierra Oaks.

Carter, R. T. (2003). Becoming racially and culturally competent: The racial-cultural counseling laboratory. *Journal of Multicultural Counseling and Development, 31.*

Caughey, J. (Ed.). (1995). *The Indians of Southern California in 1852.* Lincoln: University of Nebraska Press.

Chafee, J. (1990). *Thinking critically* (2nd ed.). Boston: Houghton Mifflin.

Chan, S. (1994). *Hmong means free: Life in Laos and America.* Philadelphia: Temple University Press.

Chattopadhyay, P. (2003). Can dissimilarity lead to positive outcomes? The influence of open versus closed minds. *Journal of Organizational Behavior, 24*(2), 295–312.

Chow, C. (1998). *Leaving deep water: Asian American women at the crossroads of two cultures.* New York: Penguin.

Chung, R. C., & Bemak, F. (2002). The relationship of culture and empathy in cross-cultural counseling. *Journal of Counseling and Development, 31,* 135–151.

Cohen, M. (1998). *Culture of intolerance.* New Haven, CT: Yale University Press.

Coleman, T. (1990, October). Managing diversity at work: The new American dilemma. *Public Management,* 1–5.

Coontz, S. (1992). *The way we never were.* New York: Basic Books.

Copeland, L. (1988, June). Valuing diversity, part 1. *Personnel,* 52–60.

Copeland, L. (1988, July). Valuing diversity, part 2. *Personnel,* 44–49.

Cox, T. (1991). The multicultural organization. *Academy of Management Executive, 5,* 34–47.

Cross, T. L. (1988). Services to minority populations: Cultural competence continuum. *Focal Point: The Bulletin of the Research and Training Center, 3*(1), 1–4.

Cryer, P. (1987). Designing an educational game, simulation or workshop: A course design perspective. *Simulation/Games for Learning, 17*(2), 51–59.

Culhane-Pera, K. A., Vawter, D. E., Xiong, P., Babbitt, B., & Solberg, M. M. (Eds.). (2003). *Healing by heart: Clinical and ethical case stories of Hmong families and western providers.* Nashville, TN: Vanderbilt University Press.

Cyrus, V. (1998). *Experiencing race, class, and gender in the United States.* Mountain View, CA: Mayfield.

Daniels, H., Bizar, M., & Zemelman, S. (2001). *Rethinking high school: Best practice in teaching, learning, and leadership.* Portsmouth, NH: Heinemann.

Davidman, L., & Davidman, P. (1994). *Teaching with a multicultural perspective: A practical guide.* New York: Longman.

Delgado, R., & Stefancic, J. (1997). *Critical white studies, looking behind the mirror.* Philadelphia: Temple University Press.

Devore, W., & Schlesinger, E. (1991). *Ethnic-sensitive social work practice.* New York: Macmillan.

DeWalt, K. M., & DeWalt, B. R. (2002). *Participant observation: A guide for fieldworkers.* Walnut Creek, CA: AltaMira Press.

Dodd, C., & Montalvo, F. (1987). *Intercultural skills for multicultural societies.* Washington, DC: Sietar International.

Dodd, M., & Taylor, S. (2005, June). Charting women of color at our winning companies. *Working Mother,* 76–92.

DuBois, E., & Ruiz, V. (1990). *Unequal sisters: A multicultural reader in U.S. women's history.* New York: Routledge.

Eddy, E., & Partridge, W. (Eds.). (1987). Theory, research and application in educational anthropology. In *Education and cultural process.* Prospect Heights, IL: Waveland Press.

Eddy, E., & Partridge, W. (Eds.). (1987). *Applied anthropology in America.* New York: Columbia University Press.

Ehrenreich, B. (1983). *The hearts of men: American dreams and flights from commitment.* Garden City, NY: Anchor Press/Doubleday.

Ehrenreich, B. (1990). *Fear of flying: The inner life of the middle class.* New York: HarperCollins.

Ehrenreich, B. (1991). *The worst days of our lives.* New York: HarperCollins.

Ehrenreich, B., & Hoschschild, A. R. (Eds.). (2002). *Global woman: Nannies, maids, and sex workers in the new economy.* New York: Henry Holt & Company.

Eisenstein, Z. (1994). *The color of gender: Reimaging democracy.* Berkeley: University of California Press.

Eisler, R. (2002). *The power of partnership.* Novato, CA: New World Library.

Eng, P. (1999). *Warrior lessons: An Asian American woman's journey into power.* New York: Pocket Books.

Essed, P. (1991). *Understanding everyday racism: An interdisciplinary theory.* Beverly Hills, CA: Sage.

Estrich, S. (2000). *Sex and power.* New York: Riverhead Books.

Ewen, L. A. (1998). *Social stratification and power in America: A view from below.* Lanham, MD: General Hall.

Feagin, J. (1999). *Racial and ethnic relations* (6th ed.). Englewood Cliffs, NJ: Prentice Hall.

Featherstone, L. (2004). *Selling women short.* New York: Basic Books.

Fernandez, J. (1991). *Managing a diverse work-force.* Lexington, MA: Lexington Books.

Ferraro, G. (1990). *The cultural dimension of international business.* Englewood Cliffs, NJ: Prentice Hall.

Fetterman, D. (1989). *Ethnography step by step.* Beverly Hills, CA: Sage.

Fine, M., Weis, L., Powell, L. C., & Wong, L. M. (1997). *Off white: Readings on race, power, and society.* New York: Routledge.

Fischer, D. (1989). *Albion's seed: Four British folkways in America.* New York: Oxford University Press.

Fitz-Gibbon, C., & Morris, L. (1987). *How to analyze data.* Newbury Park, CA: Sage.

Foley, D., & Moss, K. (2001). Studying U.S. cultural diversity: Some non-essentializing perspectives. In I. Susser & T. C. Patterson (Eds.), *Cultural diversity in the United States.* Malden, MA: Blackwell.

Foner, N., & Fredrickson, G. M. (Eds.). (2004). *Not just black and white: Historical and contemporary perspectives on immigration, race, and ethnicity in the United States.* New York: Russell Sage Foundation.

Foner, N., Rumbault, R. G., & Gold, S. J. (Eds.). (2000). *Immigration research for a new century.* New York: Russell Sage Foundation.

Fontes, L. A. (2005). *Child abuse and culture: Working with diverse families.* New York: Guildford Press.

Foster, B., et al. (1988, April). Workforce diversity and business. *Training and Development Journal,* 38–42.

Freeman, J. (1989). *Hearts of sorrow: Vietnamese-American lives.* Stanford, CA: Stanford University Press.

Furuto, S. M., Biswas, R., Chung, D., Murase, K., & Ross-Sheriff, F. (1992). *Social work practice with Asian Americans.* Newbury Park, CA: Sage.

Galanti, G. (1991). *Caring for patients from different cultures: Case studies from American hospitals.* Englewood Cliffs, NJ: Prentice Hall.

Gardenswartz, L., & Rowe, A. (1998). *Managing diversity in health care.* San Francisco: Jossey-Bass.

Gell, A. (1992). *The anthropology of time.* Providence, RI: Berg.

Gill, R., & Vazquez, C. (1996). *The Maria paradox: How Latinas can merge old world traditions with new world self-esteem.* Berkeley, CA: Perigree Books.

Glenn, E. N. (2002). *Unequal freedom: How race and gender shaped American citizenship and labor.* Cambridge, MA: Harvard University Press.

Gochenour, T. (1993). *Beyond experience: The experiential approach to cross-cultural education.* Yarmouth, ME: Intercultural Press.

Goldstein, J., & Leopold, M. (1990). Corporate culture vs. ethnic culture. *Personnel Journal,* 88–92.

Goode, J. (2001). Against cultural essentialism. In I. Susser & T. C. Patterson (Eds.), *Cultural diversity in the United States.* Malden, MA: Blackwell.

Goodenough, W. H. (1987). Multiculturalism as normal human experience. In E. Eddy & W. Partridge (Eds.), *Applied anthropology in America.* New York: Columbia University Press.

Graham, L. O. (1993). *The best companies for minorities.* New York: Penguin Books.

Green, J. (1999). *Cultural awareness in the human services.* Englewood Cliffs, NJ: Prentice Hall.

Greider, T. (1994). Theory and empowerment in cultural consultation programs. *Practicing Anthropology, 19*(3), 7–9.

Gutmann, M. (1996). *The meanings of macho.* Berkeley, CA: University of California Press.

Hall, E., & Hall, M. (1987). *Hidden differences: Doing business with the Japanese.* New York: Doubleday.

Hallowell, A. (1972). Cultural factors in the structuralization of perception. In L. Sanovar & R. Porter (Eds.), *Intercultural communication: A reader.* Belmont, CA: Wadsworth.

Hamada, Tomoko, & Sibley, Willis E. (Eds.). (1994). *Anthropological perspectives on organizational culture.* New York: University Press of America.

Handwerker, W. P. (2001). *Quick ethnography.* Walnut Creek, CA: AltaMira Press.

Hannerz, U. (1992). *Cultural complexity: Studies in the social organization of meaning.* New York: Columbia University Press.

Hannigan, T. (1990). Traits, attitudes, and skills that are related to intercultural effectiveness and their implications for cross-cultural training: A review of the literature. *International Journal of Intercultural Relations, 14,* 89–111.

Harris, P., & Moran, R. T. (1991). *Managing cultural differences.* Houston, TX: Gulf.

Harrison, B. (2001). *Collaborative programs in indigenous communities.* New York: Rowman & Littlefield.

Hart, L., & Dalke, D. (1983). *The sexes at work.* Englewood Cliffs, NJ: Prentice Hall.

Haviland, W. (2005). *Anthropology: The human challenge.* Belmont, CA: Wadsworth/Thomson.

Heizer, R. F. (Ed.). (1974/1993). *The destruction of the California indians.* Lincoln: University of Nebraska Press.

Helms, J. (1989). Considering some methodological issues in racial identity counseling research. *The Counseling Psychologist, 17,* 227–252.

Hepburn, K. S. (2004). *Building culturally and linguistically competent services to support young children, their families, and school readiness.* Baltimore: The Annie Casey Foundation.

Heyman, J. M. (2004). The anthropology of power-wielding bureaucracies. *Human Organization: Journal of the Society for Applied Anthropology, 63*(4), 487–500.

Hill-Burnett, J. (1987). Developing anthropological knowledge through application. In E. Eddy & W. Partridge (Eds.), *Applied anthropology in America.* New York: Columbia University Press.

Hite, S. (1995). *The Hite report on the family.* New York: Grove Press.

Hochschild, A. R. (1997). *The time bind: When work becomes home and home becomes work.* New York: Henry Holt & Company.

Hochschild, A. R. (2003). *The commercialization of intimate life: Notes from home and work.* London: University of California Press.

Hofstede, G. (1997). *Cultures and organization: The software of the mind.* London: McGraw-Hill.

Hogan-Garcia, M. (1991). Teaching theory and practice: A constructivist approach. *Practicing Anthropologist, 14,* 23–33.

Hogan-Garcia, M. (1994). A method for introducing the skill of cultural diversity competence in an introduction to human services course. *Journal of Counseling and Human Services Professions,* 25–43.

Hogan-Garcia, M. (1995). An anthropological approach to multicultural diversity training. *Journal of Behavioral Science, 31*(4), 490–504.

Hogan-Garcia, M., & Scheinberg, C. (2000). Culturally competent practice principles for planned interventions in organizations and communities. *Practicing Anthropology, 22*(2), 27–30.

Hogan-Garcia, M., & Wright, J. (1989). Communication and multicultural awareness: An interactional training model. *Journal of Counseling and Human Service Professions, 3*(2), 29–39.

Hogan-Garcia, M., Wright, J., & Corey, G. (1991, September/October). A multicultural perspective in an undergraduate human services program. *Journal of Counseling and Development, 70,* 86–90.

Hooks, B. (2000). *All about love: New visions.* New York: Perennial.

Hooks, B. (2003). *Teaching community: A pedagogy of hope.* New York: Routledge.

Hooks, B. (2004). *The will to change: Men, masculinity, and love.* New York: Washington Square Press.

Hudson Institute. (1987). *Workforce 2000.* Indianapolis, IN: Author.

Hughes, D., & Traughtmann, T. (1998). *Time: Histories and ethnologies.* Ann Arbor: University of Michigan Press.

Hurtado, A. L. (1988). *Indian survival on the California frontier.* New Haven, CT: Yale University Press.

Ivey, A., & Gluckstern, N. (1982). *Basic attending skills.* North Amherst, MA: Microtraining Associates.

Jamieson, D., & O'Mara, J. (1991). *Managing workforce 2000.* San Francisco: Jossey-Bass.

Johnson, M. (1992). *Simulation sourcebook.* Boulder: University of Colorado Press.

Jones, J. (1992). *The dispossessed: America's underclasses from the Civil War to the present.* New York: Basic Books.

Jordan, A. (1994). Practicing anthropology in corporate America: Consulting on organization culture. *NAPA Bulletin, 14.*

Jordan, A. T. (2003). *Business anthropology.* Prospect Heights, IL: Waveland Press.

Kanter, R. M. (1977). *Men and women of the corporation.* New York: Basic Books.

Kanter, R. M. (1983). *The change masters.* New York: Simon and Schuster.

Kanter, R. M. (1989). *When giants learn to dance.* New York: Simon and Schuster.

Kavanagh, K. H., & Kennedy, P. (1992). *Promoting cultural diversity.* Newbury Park, CA: Sage.

Keys, M., & Frank, D. (1993). *Grocery store: A role play simulation.* New York: Moorehead Kennedy Institute.

Kikumura, A. (1981). *Through harsh winters: The life of a Japanese immigrant woman.* Novato, CA: Chandler & Sharp.

Killman, R. (1987). *Beyond the quick fix.* San Francisco: Jossey-Bass.

Kleinman, A. (1988). *Rethinking psychiatry: From cultural category to personal experience.* New York: Free Press.

Knowles, M. S. (1992). *The modern practice of adult education.* New York: Basic Books.

Kochan, T., Bezrukova, K., Ely, R., Jackson, S., Joshi, A., Jehn, K., Leonard, J., Levine, D., & Thomas, D. (2003). The effects of diversity on business performance: Report of the diversity research network. *Human Resource Management, 42*(1), 3–21.

Kogod, S. (1994). The bridges process: Enhancing organizational cultures to support diversity. In A. Jordan (Ed.), Practicing anthropology in corporate America consulting on organization culture. *NAPA Bulletin, 14.*

Kohls, L. Robert. (1984). *Survival kit for overseas living.* Yarmouth, ME: Intercultural Press.

Koppelman, K. (2005). *Understanding human differences.* Boston: Pearson.

Kottak, C. P., & Kozaitis, Kathryn, A. (2003). *On being different: Diversity and multiculturalism in the North American mainstream* (2nd ed.). New York: McGraw-Hill.

Kramer, M., & Weiner, S. (1994). *Dialogues for diversity: Community and ethnicity on campus.* Phoenix, AZ: Oryx Press.

Krebs, G., & Kunimoto, E. (1994). *Effective communication in multicultural health care settings.* Thousand Oaks, CA: Sage.

Kreps, G., & Lederman, L. (1985). Using the case method in organizational communication education: Developing students' insight, knowledge, and creativity through experience-based learning and systematic debriefing. *Communication Education, 34*(4), 358–364.

Kundu, S. C. (2003). Workforce diversity status: A study of employees' reactions. *Industrial Management and Data* Systems, *103*(3–4), 215–226.

Kurowski, L. L. (2002). Cloaked culture and veiled diversity: Why theorists ignored early U.S. workforce diversity. *Management Decision, 40*(1–2), 183–191.

Lamphere, L. (Ed.). (1992). *Structuring diversity: Ethnographic perspectives on the new immigration.* Chicago: University of Chicago Press.

Lavenda, R. H., & Schultz, E. A. (2000). *Core concepts in cultural anthropology.* Mountain View, CA: Mayfield.

Lee, D. (1959). *Freedom and culture.* New York: Prentice Hall.

Lee, D. (1976). *Valuing the self: What we can learn from other cultures.* New York: Prentice Hall.

Leininger, M. (1988). Leininger's theory of nursing: Cultural care diversity and universality. *Nursing Science Quarterly,* 25–35.

Lessa, W. A., & Vogt, E. Z. (1997). *Reader in comparative religion: An anthropological approach* (4th ed.). Boston: Allyn & Bacon.

Lessa, W., & Vogt, E. (Eds.). (2000). *Reader in comparative religion, An anthropological approach.* New York: Harper & Row.

Lett, J. (1987). *The human enterprise: A critical introduction to anthropological theory.* Boulder, CO: Westview Press.

Levinson, B., Foley, D., & Holland, D. (1996). *The cultural production of the educated person.* New York: State University of New York Press.

Leviton, S., & Greenstone, J. (1997). *Elements of mediation.* Pacific Grove, CA: Brooks/Cole.

Lieberman, Leonard. (1997). *"Race" 1997 and 2001: A race odyssey.* Arlington, VA: American Anthropological Association, GAD Module Series in Teaching Anthropology, Module 3.

Lieberman, Leonard, & Rice, Patricia C. (1996). *Race or clines?* Arlington, VA: American Anthropological Association, GAD Module Series in Teaching Anthropology, Module 2.

Liu, E. (1998). *The accidental Asian.* New York: Random House.

Locke, D. (1992). *Increasing multicultural understanding.* Newbury Park, CA: Sage.

Loden, M. (1996). *Implementing diversity.* Chicago: Irwin.

Loden, M., & Rosener, J. (1991). *Workforce America! Managing employee diversity as a vital resource.* Homewood, IL: Business One Irwin.

Longstreet, W. (1978). *Aspects of ethnicity.* New York: Teachers College Press.

Lum, D. (1992, 2000). *Social work practice and people of color.* Pacific Grove, CA: Brooks/Cole.

Mackelprang, R., & Salsgiver, R. (1999). *Disability: A diversity model approach in human service practice.* Pacific Grove, CA: Brooks/Cole.

Malott, R., Tillema, M., & Glenn, S. (1978). *Behavior analysis and behavior modification: An introduction.* Grand Rapids, MI: Behaviordelia.

Marcus, G., & Fischer, M. (1986). *Anthropology as cultural critique.* Chicago: University of Chicago Press.

Marks, J. (2005). The profound relevance and irrelevance of biology. *General Anthropology, 11*(2), 1–7.

McCann, N., & McGinn, T. (1992). *Harassed: 100 women define inappropriate behavior in the workplace.* Homewood, IL: Business One Irwin.

McDermott, R. (1987). Achieving school failure: An anthropological approach to illiteracy and social stratification. In G. Spindler (Ed.), *Education and cultural process.* Prospect Heights, IL: Waveland Press.

McGoldrick, M., Pearce, J. K., & Giordano, J. (1982). *Ethnicity and family therapy.* New York: Guilford Press.

McGrath, P., & Axelson, J. (1993). *Accessing awareness and developing knowledge: Foundations for skill in a multicultural society.* Pacific Grove, CA: Brooks/Cole.

McIntosh, Peggy. (1993). Examining unearned privilege. *On Campus with Women, 22,* 9–10.

McKinney, K. D. (2005). *Being white: Stories of race and racism.* New York: Routledge.

Meador, Elizabeth. (2005). The making of marginality: Schooling for Mexican immigrant girls in the rural southwest. *Anthropology and Education Quarterly, 36,* 149–164.

Meeks, K. (2000). *Driving while black.* New York: Broadway Books.

Mehr, J. (1992/2004). *Human services concepts and intervention strategies.* Boston: Allyn & Bacon.

Mental Health Services Act (MHSA). (2005). Mental Health Services Act Community Services and Supports. Three Year Program and Expenditure Plan Requirements, Fiscal years 2005–2008. California Department of Mental Health, May 18, 2005.

Merry, S. (2001). Racialized identities and the law. In I. Susser & T. C. Patterson (Eds.), *Cultural diversity in the United States.* Malden, MA: Blackwell.

Montagu, A. (1974). *The concept of race* (2nd ed.). New York: Free Press.

Montgomery, C. L. (1993). *Healing through communication.* Newbury Park, CA: Sage.

Morgan, G., & Ramirez, R. (1983). Action learning: A holographic metaphor for guiding social change. *Human Relations, 37,* 1–28.

Morrison, A. (1992). *The new leaders: Guidelines on leadership diversity in America.* San Francisco: Jossey-Bass.

Multicultural education. (1993, September). *Phi Delta Kappan.*

Nader, L. (Ed.). (1994). *Essays on controlling processes.* Berkeley, CA: Kroeber Anthropological Society Papers (77).

Nader, L. (Ed.). (1996). *Naked science: Anthropological inquiry into boundaries, power and knowledge.* New York: Routledge.

Nash, J. (2001). Labor struggles: Gender, ethnicity, and the new migration. In I. Susser & T. C. Patterson (Eds.), *Cultural diversity in the United States.* Malden, MA: Blackwell.

Nebelkopf, E., & Phillips, M. (Eds.). (2004). *Healing and mental health for Native Americans: Speaking in red.* Walnut Creek, CA: AltaMira Press.

Nelson, S. (1988, July). Meet your new work-force. *Nation's Business,* 14–21.

Neukrug, E. (1994). *Theory, practice, and trends in human services: An overview of an emerging profession.* Pacific Grove, CA: Brooks/Cole.

Ore, T. (2000). *The social construction of difference and inequality.* Mountain View, CA: Mayfield.

Orque, M., Bloch, B., & Monroy, L. (1983). *Ethnic nursing care: A multicultural approach.* St. Louis: C. V. Mosby.

Orta, A. (2004). The promise of particularism and the theology of culture: Limits and lesson of "neo-Boasianism." *American Anthropologist, 106*(3), 473–487.

Padilla, A. (1986). Acculturation and stress among immigrants and later generation individuals. In *The quality of urban life.* New York: Russell Sage Foundation.

Paige, R. Michael. (1993). *Education for the intercultural experience.* Yarmouth, ME: Intercultural Press.

Pandian, J. (2002). *Supernaturalism in human life: A discourse in myth, ritual and religion*. Pitampura, New Delhi: Vedams.

Parkin, R., & Stone, L. (Eds.). (2004). *Kinship and family: An anthropological reader*. Malden, MA: Blackwell.

Partridge, W. (1987). Toward a theory of practice. In E. Eddy & W. Partridge, *Applied anthropology in America*. New York: Columbia University Press.

Paul, R. (1990). *Critical thinking: What every person needs to survive in a rapidly changing world*. Rohnert Park, CA: Sonoma State University.

Pederson, P. (1988). *A handbook for developing multicultural awareness*. Alexandria, VA: American Association for Counseling and Development.

Pederson, P. (1989). Developing multicultural ethical guidelines for psychology. *International Journal of Psychology, 24*, 1–11.

Pederson, P. (1990). The multicultural perspective as a fourth force in counseling. *Journal of Mental Health Counseling, 12*(1), 93–95.

Petranak, C., Corey, S., & Black, R. (1992). Three levels of learning in simulations: Participating, debriefing, and journal writing. *Simulation and Gaming, 23*(2), 174–185.

Phinney, J. (1989, May). Stages of ethnic identity development in minority group adolescents. *Journal of Early Adolescence, 9*(1–2), 34–49.

Phinney, J. (1990). Ethnic identity in adolescents and adults: Review of research. *Psychological Bulletin, 108*(3), 499–514.

Phinney, J., & Rotherman, M. (1987). *Children's ethnic socialization*. Newbury Park, CA: Sage.

Portes, A. (1996). *The new second generation*. New York: Russell Sage Foundation.

Powell, G. (1988). *Women and men in management*. Newbury Park, CA: Sage.

Powell, G. (1994). *Gender and diversity in the work place*. Thousand Oaks, CA: Sage.

Prosser, M. (1989). *The cultural dialogue: An introduction to intercultural communication*. Washington DC: SEITAR International.

Rhinesmith, S. H. (1993). *A manager's guide to globalization*. Alexandria, VA: American Society for Training and Development.

Richard, O., McMillian, A., Chadwick, K., & Dwyer, K. (2003). Employing an innovation strategy in racially diverse workforces: Effects on firm performance. *Group and Organization Management, 28*(1).

Rivera, F., & Erlich, J. (1998). *Community organizing in a diverse society*. Boston: Allyn & Bacon.

Roediger, David R. (1991). *The wages of whiteness*. New York: Verso.

Root, M. (1985). Guidelines for facilitating therapy with Asian American clients. *Psychotherapy, 22*, 349–356.

Root, M. (1992). *Racially mixed people in America*. Newbury Park, CA: Sage.

Rosaldo, J. W. (1986). Toward an interfacing of Hispanic cultural variables with school psychology service delivery systems. *Professional Psychology: Research and Practice, 17*, 191–199.

Rose, D. (1990). *Living the ethnographic life*. Newbury Park, CA: Sage.

Rosen, R. (1991). *The healthy company: Eight strategies to develop people, productivity, and products*. New York: Putnam.

Rosenblatt, D. (2004). An anthropology made safe for culture: Patterns of practice and the politics of difference in Ruth Benedict. *American Anthropologist, 106*(3), 459–472.

Rosener, J. (1998). *America's competitive secret: Women managers*. New York: Oxford University Press.

Rosenholtz, S. J. (1991). *Teacher's workplace. The social organization of schools*. New York: Teachers College Columbia University Press.

Ruby, J. (1982). *A crack in the mirror: Reflexive perspectives in anthropology*. Philadelphia: University of Pennsylvania Press.

Sanday, Peggy R. (1979). The ethnographic paradigm(s). *Administrative Science Quarterly, 24*, 527–538.

Sapir, E. (1927). The unconscious patterning of behavior in society. In E. S. Dummer (Ed.), *The unconscious: A symposium*. New York: Knopf.

Saravia-Shore, M., & Arvizu, S. (1992). *Cross-cultural literacy ethnographies of communication in multiethnic classrooms*. New York: Garland.

Schein, E. (1996). Culture: The missing concept in organization studies. *Administrative Science Quarterly, 41*, 229–240.

Schon, D. (1987). *Educating the reflective practitioner*. San Francisco: Jossey-Bass.

Schultz, D. (1993). *To reclaim a legacy of diversity: Analyzing the "political correctness" debates in higher education*. New York: National Council for Research on Women.

Schultz, F. (1994). *Multicultural education*. Guilford, CT: Duskin.

Schwartz, T. (1978). Where is culture? Personality as the distributive locus of culture. In G. Spindler (Ed.), *The making of psychological anthropology*. Berkeley: University of California Press.

Schwartzman, Helen B. (1993). *Ethnography in organizations.* Newbury Park, CA: Sage.

Sherman, V. C. (1993). *Creating the new American hospital.* San Francisco: Jossey-Bass.

Shipek, F. C. (1991). *Delfina Cuero: Her autobiography and account of her last years and her ethnobotanic contributions.* Menlo Park, CA: Ballena Press.

Sidel, R. (1978). *Urban survival: The world of working class women.* Lincoln: University of Nebraska Press.

Sikkema, M., & Niyekawa, A. (1987). *Design for cross-cultural learning.* Yarmouth, ME: Intercultural Press.

Simons, G., Vazquez, C., & Harris, P. R. (1993). *Transcultural leadership: Empowering the diverse workforce.* Houston, TX: Gulf.

Sims, H. P., & Lorenzi, P. (1992). *The leadership paradigm.* Newbury Park, CA: Sage.

Sleeter, C., & McLaren, P. (1995). *Multicultural education, critical pedagogy, and the politics of difference.* New York: State University of New York Press.

Smith, T. (1993). *Parzival's briefcase: Six practices and a new philosophy for healthy organizational change.* San Francisco: Chronicle Books.

Snowden, L. R., & Cheung, F. K. (1990). Use of inpatient mental health services by members of ethnic minority groups. *American Psychologist, 45,* 347–355.

Spector, R. E. (1991). *Cultural diversity in health and illness.* San Mateo, CA: Appleton & Lange.

Spector, R. E. (2000). *Cultural diversity in health and illness.* Upper Saddle River, NJ: Prentice Hall Health.

Spindler, G. (1982). *Doing the ethnography of schooling.* Prospect Heights, IL: Waveland Press.

Spindler, G. (1987). *Education and cultural process.* Prospect Heights, IL: Waveland Press.

Starr, K., & Orsi, R. J. (Eds.). (2000). *Rooted in barbarous soil: People, culture, and community in gold rush California.* London: University of California Press.

Stewart, E., & Bennet, M. (1991). *American cultural patterns.* Yarmouth, ME: Intercultural Press.

Stone, L. (Ed.). (2001). *New directions in anthropological kinship.* Lanham, MD: Rowman & Littlefield.

Strober, E. (2005). "Is power-sharing possible?" Using empowerment evaluation with parents and nurses in a pediatric hospital transplantation setting. *Human Organization: Journal of the Society for Applied Anthropology, 64*(2), 201–210.

Sue, D. (1981). *Counseling the culturally different.* New York: John Wiley & Sons.

Sue, D., & Sue S. (1987). Cultural factors in the clinical assessment of Asian Americans. *Journal of Consulting and Clinical Psychology, 55,* 479–487.

Susser, I. (2001). Poverty and homelessness in U.S. cities. In I. Susser & T. C. Patterson (Eds.), *Cultural diversity in the United States.* Malden, MA: Blackwell.

Susser, I., & Patterson, T. (Eds.). (2001). *Cultural diversity in the United States.* Malden, MA: Blackwell.

Tannen, D. (1990). *You just don't understand: Women and men in conversation.* New York: Ballentine Books.

Tatum, B. D. (1993). Talking about race, learning about racism: The application of racial identity development theory in the classroom. *Harvard Educational Review, 62*(1), 1–24.

Tatum, B. D. (1997). *Why are all the black kids sitting together in the cafeteria?* New York: Basic Books.

Thatcher, E. (1990, September). Promoting learning through games and simulations. *Simulation and Gaming,* 262–273.

Thiederman, S. (1991). *Bridging the cultural barriers for corporate success.* Lexington, MA: Lexington Books.

Thomas, R. Roosevelt. (1996). *Redefining diversity.* New York: American Management Association.

Tylor, E. (1958). *Primitive culture,* Vol. I. New York: Harper & Row.

U.S. Department of Labor. (1991). *The glass ceiling report.* Washington, DC: Government Publications.

Van Ments, M. (1992). Role playing without tears—some problems of using role-play. *Simulations/Games for Learning, 22*(2), 82–90.

Walck, Christa L., & Jordan, Ann T. (Eds.). (1995). Special issue: Managing diversity: Anthropology's contribution to theory and practice. *Journal of Applied Behavioral Science, 31,* 1–247.

Wali, Alaka, & Khan, Naveeda. (1997). Inserting "culture" into multiculturalism, conversations at the Field Museum, Chicago. *Anthropology Today, 13*(4) 9–12.

Ward, M. C. (1998). *A sounding of women: Autobiographies from unexpected places.* Needham Heights, MA: Allyn & Bacon.

Watkins, K. E., & Marshack, V. J. (1993). *Sculpting the learning organization.* San Francisco: Jossey-Bass.

Weatherford, J. (1991). *Native roots: How the Indians enriched America.* New York: Crown.

Whyte, W. F. (1987). Organizational behavior research: Changing styles of research and action. In E. Eddy & W. Partridge (Eds.), *Applied anthropology in America.* New York: Columbia University Press.

Wilson, B. D., & Caughey, J. W. (Eds.). (1995). *The Indians of southern California in 1852.* Lincoln: University of Nebraska Press.

Winkelman, M. (1999). *Ethnic sensitivity in social work.* Dubuque, IA: Eddie Bowers.

Winkelman, M. (2001). Ethnicity and psychocultural models. In I. Susser & T. C. Patterson (Eds.), *Cultural diversity in the United States.* Malden, MA: Blackwell.

Winkelman, M. (2005). *Cultural awareness, sensitivity and competence.* Peosta, IA: Eddie Bowers.

Wise, T. (2005). *White like me.* New York: Soft Skull Press.

Wiseman R., Hammer, M., & Nishida, H. (1989). Predictors of intercultural communication competence. *International Journal of Intercultural Relations, 13,* 349–370.

Wolcott, H. F. (1999). *Ethnography: A way of seeing.* Walnut Creek, CA: AltaMira Press.

Wright, Susan. (1994). *Anthropology of organizations.* New York: Routledge.

Wulff, R., & Fiske, S. (1987). *Anthropological praxis: Translating knowledge into action.* Boulder, CO: Westview Press.

Zack, N. (1995). *American mixed race: The culture of microdiversity.* Lanham, MD: Rowman & Littlefield.

Zane, N. W., Takeuchi, D. T., & Young, K. (Eds.). (1994). *Confronting critical health issues of Asian and Pacific Islander Americans.* Thousand Oaks, CA: Sage.

Index